THE MOST IMPORTANT PERSON ON EARTH

STUDY GUIDE

The Holy Spirit,
Governor of the Kingdom

DR. MYLES MUNROE

WHITAKER
HOUSE

THE MOST IMPORTANT PERSON ON EARTH STUDY GUIDE
workbook edition

Dr. Myles Munroe
Bahamas Faith Ministries International
P.O. Box N9583
Nassau, Bahamas
e-mail: bfmadmin@bfmmm.com
websites: www.bfmmm.com; www.bfmi.tv; www.mylesmunroe.tv

ISBN: 978-0-88368-197-8
Printed in the United States of America
© 2007 by Dr. Myles Munroe

1030 Hunt Valley Circle
New Kensington, PA 15068
www.whitakerhouse.com

Library of Congress Cataloging-in-Publication Data

Munroe, Myles.
The most important person on earth study guide / Myles Munroe.
p. cm.
Summary: "This study guide to *The Most Important Person on Earth: The Holy Spirit, Governor of the Kingdom* is designed for personal application to give readers a deeper understanding of why the Holy Spirit is the key to their purpose and fulfillment on earth"—Provided by publisher.
ISBN 978-0-88368-197-8 (pbk. : alk. paper) 1. Holy Spirit—Textbooks. I. Title.
BT121.3.M862 2007
231'.3—dc22
2007016891

1 2 3 4 5 6 7 8 9 10 11 12 ⊞ 15 14 13 12 11 10 09 08 07

CONTENTS

HOW TO USE THIS STUDY GUIDE

This study guide complement to *The Most Important Person on Earth: The Holy Spirit, Governor of the Kingdom* by Dr. Myles Munroe may be used by individuals or groups and can be easily adapted to suit the needs of either. For your convenience, an answer key is provided in the back of this study guide.

Each chapter review includes the following elements:

Chapter Theme: The main idea of each chapter is summarized for emphasis and clarity.

Questions for Reflection: One or more questions are given as a warm-up to lead into the study or discussion of the topic. (For group study, these questions may be asked before or after reading the Chapter Theme, at the leader's discretion.)

Exploring Principles and Purposes: Questions and review material are provided to highlight and summarize the truths and principles within each chapter and begin to lead the reader/group participant to personalize what is being studied. Page numbers corresponding to the book are listed for easy reference.

Conclusion: A summary or implication statement is included, helping the reader/group member to put the chapter into perspective according to the overall theme of the book.

Applying the Principles of Kingdom Living: Thought-provoking questions as well as suggestions for personal action and prayer are provided to help the individual/group participant apply the study material to his or her particular life circumstances. This section includes three parts:

- Thinking It Over
- Acting on It
- Praying about It

As you progress through *The Most Important Person on Earth* and review its principles through this study guide, you will discover in a deeper way why the Holy Spirit is heaven's Governor on earth and the key to your fulfillment and potential. Under the Governor's guidance and enabling, you will become a true representative of the kingdom—not only entering into his purpose and power for your life, but also bringing hope, healing, and power to others in the name of the King.

INTRODUCTION

The greatest dream in the heart of every human being is of a perfect world. The greatest desire and pursuit of all humankind is the power to achieve this dream. We all want power, which is the ability and capacity to control circumstances and destiny.

Yet it often seems as if the state of the world today is one of ongoing crises, so that many people are asking, "Who's in charge?" We want to know how to solve our global problems, such as terrorist attacks, war, crime, hunger, AIDS, flu epidemics, and economic instability. We want to find out who has the authority and the ability to solve the problems, bring stability, and maintain a peaceful and prosperous life.

Our inability to find real solutions to problems is often mirrored in our personal lives, as well. When financial setbacks arise, our personal dreams are dashed, or our children seem bent on self-destruction, we ask ourselves, in effect, "Who's in control?" We certainly don't feel as if we are. We long to create order and peace and well-being in our families once more.

We desire the authority and the power to change our circumstances. This is why I'm convinced that the number one desire of all people in every situation of life—global or personal—is for *power*. Power is *the ability to influence and control circumstances.*

Power is therefore the principle issue of humanity. People may not express it in exactly that way, but ultimately they desire the ability to manage and shape their circumstances, reverse personal and family setbacks, and build a better life for themselves. It makes no difference what gender, financial status, or ethnicity a person may have; everyone desires to influence his life and the world around him. And the frequent lack of this influence is frustrating and painful.

The chaos in our world and the uncertain nature of our individual lives reveals the absence of authority and power that can address our deepest needs and most critical issues. This is the reason many of us admire and try to emulate the talented, powerful, and influential; this is also why we seek to cultivate a sense of hope and faith in the noble qualities of humanity.

It is also interesting to note that some of our most popular fictional superheroes have their origins in another world or distant planet. This may indicate that, deep in the heart of mankind, there is an unconscious awareness that the solution to our earthly dilemma cannot come from our planet itself. Rather, our help must come from another realm.

There are solutions for the problems and crises in our families, communities, businesses, nations, and world. As a planet under siege, we need help from a higher authority, help from a greater world that has the ability to address our needs. We need someone from that world who has experience in bringing light into darkness, life into barrenness, and order out of chaos. If we could identify that person, and he came to earth to solve all our problems, he would naturally be called the most important person on earth. Only one person has those qualifications. Actually, he is already here on earth. We must meet him, come to understand him, and discover his purpose, intent, program, and strategy to enable us to regain our authority and power, and to influence life on earth as we were meant to.

—*Dr. Myles Munroe*

Part 1

THE PROGRAM OF CELESTIAL EXPANSION

Chapter One

THE POWER OF INFLUENCE

CHAPTER THEME

The role of the governor in a traditional kingdom is central to our understanding of the relationship between a kingdom and its colony. This knowledge has implications for us concerning what it means to live the "kingdom life." The kingdom life is not a political system or a particular national government; it far transcends the aspirations and fortunes of individual earthly empires. It is a way of understanding and living everyday life that applies to people of every race and creed on earth. It gives us a deep understanding of our true nature as human beings, while revealing the key to our remarkable life purpose and enabling us to exercise our full potential in the world.

Questions for Reflection

1. What form of civil government do you live under? What are the general responsibilities of the leaders to the people, and vice versa?

2. How would you define the office of governor under your style of government?

3. Would you rather live under a kingdom or under a republic/democracy? Why?

Exploring Principles and Purposes

4. What does the success of your life depend on, according to Dr. Munroe's investigation into the concept of kingdom? (p. 27)

5. Why is the contemporary world generally anti-kingdom? (p. 28)

6. What arenas of life does the anti-kingdom perspective affect? (p. 28)

7. What essential questions does the transcendent "kingdom life" answer for people of all nations, religions, and creeds? (p. 29)

8. You are meant to find yourself in a relationship between _____ and _____. (p. 29)

9. What effect does the transcendent kingdom have on humanity as opposed to the political kingdoms of the past and present? (p. 29)

10. What principal issue of humanity does the kingdom life address? How is this issue defined? (p. 30)

11. What is Dr. Munroe's definition of kingdom? (p. 30)

12. In a true, traditional kingdom, all _____ is vested in the _____. (p. 30)

13. What is the job of a king's advisors? (p. 31)

14. What is the goal of a traditional kingdom? (p. 31)

15. The home country of a king is his _____, and the outlying territories are his _____. (p. 31)

16. What is a sovereign's number one goal after gaining a colony? (p. 31)

17. What was the word *colony* derived from in the Latin? (p. 32)

18. List the four purposes of a colony: (p. 32)

    (1)

    (2)

    (3)

    (4)

19. The royal governor was… [choose one] (p. 34)

    (a) to supersede the absent king in the colony.

    (b) the presence of the absent king in the colony.

    (c) better than the absent king for the colony.

    (d) independent of the king in the colony.

20. What made the governor the most important person in a colony? (p. 35)

21. Match the six purposes of a governor with their significance: (p. 35)

   (1) *relationship*   (4) *interpretation*

   (2) *communication*   (5) *power*

   (3) *representation*   (6) *partnership*

Clarifies the king's desires, ideas, intent, purposes, will, and plans: _____

Conveys what the king wants the colony to know or receive: _____

Shares rule with the king: _____

Provides the kingdom access to the colony: _____

Acts on behalf of the king to the colony, and on behalf of the colony to the king:

_____

Exercises authority to execute the king's desires and commands for the colony.

_____

For questions 22–30, circle True or False regarding the royal governor's qualifications and roles:

22. The royal governor was appointed by the king. (p. 36)   True   False

23. The governor was chosen from among the people of the colony. (p. 36)   True   False

24. The royal governor was accountable to both king and people. (p. 36)   True   False

25. The governor was not in the colony to promote his own personal policies or agendas. (p. 36)   True   False

26. The governor's job was to exchange the culture of the territory for the culture of the kingdom. (p. 37)   True   False

27. The colonists were to take on the culture but not the history of the kingdom. (p. 37)   True   False

28. Colonists were automatically granted the full rights of citizens. (pp. 37–39)   True   False

29. The governor lived in the kingdom but visited the colony periodically to carry out his responsibilities for the king. (p. 39)   True   False

30. The governor left if the colony declared independence. (p. 39)   True   False

31. List several reasons the governor was of great value to the colony. (p. 40)

32. What statement did Jesus of Nazareth make about a kingdom that transcends human governments and speaks to the basis of our very nature and existence as human beings? (p. 41)

33. Jesus was announcing the _____ return of a kingdom and its _____ on earth. (p. 41)

34. What properties does the transcendent kingdom have in relation to traditional earthly kingdoms? (p. 41)

Conclusion

When a kingdom takes a territory, its goal is to make that territory exactly like the kingdom. The purpose is to transform the colony so it mirrors the home country in its mind-set and lifestyle, its characteristics and culture. The transformation of a colony into the culture of the kingdom doesn't happen automatically. A purposeful development is involved. The king administers his will through his personal representative, the governor, who is the presence of the absent king in the colony. With the governor in the colony, the colonists do not need the actual physical presence of the king to experience and be changed by the king's influence.

Jesus of Nazareth made a significant statement about the return of a kingdom and its influence on earth. This kingdom has properties that are similar to, but go beyond, the traditional kingdoms we have examined in this chapter.

Applying the Principles of Kingdom Living

Thinking It Over

• What is your perspective on kingdoms? Would you say you have a pro- or anti-kingdom perspective? Why?

• What kingdom do you think Jesus of Nazareth was referring to? What do you think is the nature of this kingdom?

Acting on It

• Do a search of the various references Jesus made to *kingdom* in the accounts of his life in the Scriptures. (See the first four books of the New Testament, also called the Gospels. A Bible concordance [topical index] or a computer Bible program is a good way to do this.)

• What do you learn about the transcendent kingdom from these statements?

THE SUCCESS OF YOUR LIFE DEPENDS UPON HOW WELL YOU LIVE OUT THE KINGDOM LIFE.

Chapter Two

THE ADAMIC ADMINISTRATION

CHAPTER THEME

The eternal King of the invisible world desired to expand his heavenly domain as an extension of himself and his government. He created the earth as additional territory for him to rule and transform into the expression of his nature and desires. He did not rule this territory directly, however. The Creator-King created human beings as his beloved offspring, his royal children, and delegated rule of the earth to them. The specific nature of their creation and their connection to their King and Father was crucial to their ability to carry out their assignment.

Questions for Reflection

1. How would you describe human beings' basic nature and characteristics?

2. Do human beings have a purpose on earth? If so, what is it?

Exploring Principles and Purposes

3. Where did the first government on earth come from? (p. 43)

4. In what ways is the transcendent kingdom different from a traditional earthly kingdom? (p. 43)

    (1)

    (2)

    (3)

5. In what ways is the transcendent kingdom similar to a traditional kingdom? (p. 44)

    (1)

    (2)

6. How did the physical universe come into being? (p. 44)

7. To whom does the universe belong? (p. 44)

8. What maintains the universe? (p. 45)

9. The King of the _____ world decided to create a _____ world. (pp. 45–46)

10. What is the definition of the invisible, transcendent kingdom, based on Dr. Munroe's definition of kingdom from chapter one? (p. 46)

11. Heaven is God's _____ or _____ _____ and earth is his _____. (p. 46)

12. What nature were human beings created to have? (p. 47)

13. What did the Creator-King extend to human beings after creating them in his own image and likeness? (p. 47)

14. What do the words *image* (essential nature) and *likeness* (the original after which a thing is patterned) tell us about who we are as human beings? (pp. 47–48)

15. What is the only way a kingdom can function perfectly? (p. 48)

16. The key to a true kingdom is _____. (p. 48)

17. A perfect government exists for... [choose one] (p. 48)

    (a) itself

    (b) the ruler

    (c) its citizens

    (d) its prosperity

18. What two things did the Creator-King give human beings so they could fulfill their rulership of the earth? (p. 48)

    (1)

    (2)

19. In what three ways did the breath of the Spirit ignite life in Adam? (p. 49)

    (1)

    (2)

    (3)

20. What did man's soul and body give him an awareness of? (p. 49)

21. What did man's spirit—through the Spirit of God dwelling within him—give him an awareness of? (p. 49)

22. The Creator's Spirit within humanity was our heavenly "_____" on earth, who _____ from the King and _____ with us in the colony of earth. (p. 49)

23. What did the Creator's Spirit, the Governor, enable humanity to do? (p. 49)

24. The nature of the Creator-King was to be first communicated through… [choose one] (p. 49)

    (a) man's spirit

    (b) man's soul

    (c) man's physical body

25. What is the true, kingdom-built residence in which the Governor lives and governs the colony of earth? (p. 50)

26. True or False: [circle one] (p. 50)

    Human beings were created as subjects of the kingdom.

27. What is the assignment of the Adamic Administration? (p. 51)

28. Define what it means to have dominion. (p. 51)

29. Describe humanity's basic job description on earth. (p. 52)

30. What was the key to human beings' effective rulership of earth? (p. 52)

31. In what ways did the Governor fulfill the requirements of delegated authority for human beings—an open channel of communication to the king and the power to perform their responsibilities in accordance with the king's wishes? (p. 52)

32. Why were human beings suited to implement the transformation of the colony of earth into the nature of the heavenly kingdom? (pp. 52–53)

33. The Holy Spirit, as Governor of the human spirit, was humanity's _____ to the home kingdom; he was the direct _____ of _____ between the spirit of man and the government of heaven. (p. 53)

34. What two things did the presence of the Holy Spirit within human beings provide them? What primary issue of humanity do these address? (p. 53)

35. Why do human beings ultimately desire power, the ability to influence and control circumstances? (p. 53)

36. The message of the creation of humanity is… [choose all that apply] (p. 54)

    (a) practical

    (b) about performing rituals

    (c) the rule of an eternal King over his territory

    (d) about religion

    (e) the relationship between a King and his ruler-children

    (f) the transformation of colony into kingdom

Conclusion

The Creator-King made human beings according to his own nature—his image and likeness. He also placed his own Spirit within them to personally guide and enable them to remain connected to his purposes and will, while having authority and power to carry out their dominion rule of the earth. It was only through the indwelling of the Creator's Spirit, the Governor, that humanity could fulfill its mandate of transforming the earth into a replica of the heavenly kingdom.

Applying the Principles of Kingdom Living

Thinking It Over

- Has your thinking about the nature of God and humanity changed after reading this chapter? If so, in what way?

- To what extent are you living out humanity's purpose of transforming the earth into a replica of the heavenly kingdom?

- How much influence do you allow the Spirit of God—the Governor—to have in your life?

Acting on It

- What aspects of the nature of the kingdom would you like to develop in your life?

- List two ways in which your daily activities could better fulfill humanity's purpose of cultivating the earth according to the nature of the kingdom.

Praying about It

- Dr. Munroe said human beings are designed to live from the "inside out" rather than the "outside in." We are meant to be led by the Spirit of God in our spirits. This leading is to be manifested through our souls—mind, will, and emotions—and eventually find expression through our physical bodies. Ask God to help you live your life according to His Spirit so you may fulfill your purpose on earth.

WE WERE DESIGNED TO BE LIKE AND FUNCTION LIKE THE RULER OF THE INVISIBLE KINGDOM.

NOTES

Chapter Three

DECLARATION OF INDEPENDENCE

CHAPTER THEME

The King had created the territory of earth, and the colony had been established. The King's children were provided with a rich home and given authority to rule and prosper on earth in behalf of their Father, through the Governor who dwelled within them. The heavenly kingdom's plan of expanding the nature of its realm on earth was interrupted, however, by an intruder. This put into effect a series of events that subjugated the King's children and the colony of earth, severing their connection with the King and destroying their ability to govern the world.

Questions for Reflection

1. Have you ever believed a lie? What impact did it have on your life?

2. In what ways is independence a positive concept? In what ways might it be a negative one?

Exploring Principles and Purposes

3. What happened to disrupt the heavenly kingdom's plan of expanding its realm on earth? (p. 55)

4. Who instigated this disruption in the plan, and what was his motivation for doing so? (pp. 55–56)

5. What was the nature of Lucifer's plan for disrupting the colony? (p. 56)

6. What was the strategy for accomplishing it? (p. 56)

7. The King's explicit instructions for his children, which they rejected, had been instituted... [choose one] (p. 57)

    (a) for the children's protection

    (b) to subordinate them

    (c) to make them weak

    (d) to make the King feel important

8. In what two ways were the disbelief and rebellion of the King's children toward the King unnatural? (p. 57)

    (1)

    (2)

9. The rebellion of the King's children represented a _____ _____ _____ and _____ from the heart and will of the King. (p. 57)

10. What did the children's rebellion ultimately amount to? (pp. 57–58)

11. According to the nature of the kingdom, what is the definition of sin? (p. 58)

12. The King's children handed over the colony of earth to the King's enemy. What would Lucifer transform the colony into? (p. 58)

13. What was the worst result of the children's rejection of the King and his nature? (p. 59)

14. How did this loss affect the spirits, souls, and bodies of human beings? (pp. 59–60)

15. Governors in traditional human kingdoms are forced out or are called to withdraw if a colony becomes independent from the mother country. Likewise, when humanity declared independence, the Governor was _____ to the heavenly kingdom. (p. 60)

16. How did the environment of earth change with the loss of the Governor? (p. 62)

17. Although human beings were designed to live from the _____ _____, the loss of the Spirit caused them to live from the _____ _____. (p. 62)

18. What did human beings become dependent on after they lost the Spirit? (pp. 62–63)

19. Living mainly by a sensual perspective rather than a spiritual one gave humanity… [choose one] (p. 63)

    (a) a clearer view of life

    (b) freedom to be who they really were

    (c) a limited perspective on life's realities

    (d) more knowledge about the world

20. Why is it dangerous to interpret the physical world only from the physical world itself? (pp. 63–64)

21. List several reasons why the Governor is the key to our being fully human. (p. 64)

22. In addition to losing communication with the home country, human beings also lost the _____ and _____ the Governor provided. (p. 64)

23. From the King's standpoint, what was the result of the children's self-government? (pp. 65–66)

24. For humanity, what were the harsh realities of self-government? (p. 66)

25. What state were human beings left in after losing the Governor? (p. 66)

26. What has this state done to the image and nature of the Creator within us, as well as our attempts at government on earth? (pp. 66–67)

27. Describe the culture human beings created as a substitute for the culture of heaven. (p. 67)

28. What was the result of humanity's attempts to dominate the King's colony without the mind and heart of the King? (p. 68)

29. Immediately following humanity's rebellion and the loss of the Governor, the King... [choose one] (p. 69)

    (a) believed humanity was not worth saving

    (b) told humanity to figure out its own problems

    (c) said Lucifer and humanity deserved one another

    (d) promised the return of the Governor and earth's restoration

30. What is the bottom line in every person's search for power and meaning in life? (pp. 69–70)

31. What was the King's plan to restore the Governor to earth? (p. 69)

32. A human being without the Governor is _____ because he's never _____. (p. 70)

Conclusion

The rebellion of human beings against their Creator-King is often referred to as "the fall" because of the extreme change in the quality of existence humanity experienced. It was like a prince falling from a luxurious royal coach into a muddy ditch and then having to live there. Humanity's independence from heaven's kingdom is the worst thing that ever happened to human beings, whereas the kingdom was the best thing they could have been given.

Humanity's rebellion and self-government was not the triumph of freedom over tyranny. It was not a removal of the shackles of foreign occupation. It was like rejecting a beloved family, home country, and billion-dollar inheritance all at once. The recall of the Governor was a devastating loss to the inhabitants of earth, who now experienced sorrow, pain, and death as common occurrences of the world they now lived in. The greatest tragedy of all was the loss of the King's Spirit within them. Without the Governor, they no longer had a direct connection to the King or the authority and power necessary for ruling the colony of earth.

Applying the Principles of Kingdom Living

Thinking It Over

- Have you had a sense something is missing in your life, though you haven't known what it is? What have you used to try to fill the emptiness (for example, money, relationships, work, parties, sports)? How would the presence of the Governor in your life remove the emptiness you have experienced?

- In what ways are you interpreting life through your physical senses rather than by the nature and Spirit of the Creator-King?

- Are there any areas in your life where you have believed the lie from Lucifer that being independent from the Creator-King is a good thing? How would a full reconnection with Him change your life for the better?

Acting on It

- Dr. Munroe wrote that "sin is rebellion against the essential nature and authority of the heavenly government." Think about a sin you are currently struggling with and describe how it is in opposition to the nature and authority of the King.

- List several things you know God expects of you, based on Scripture, but which you have felt were restrictive. Then write how the apparent restrictions are for your protection.

Praying about It

- Honestly admit to the Creator-King if you have been living a life (even parts of it) independent from him. Recognize this not only hurts you but grieves his heart, since he only wants the best for you. Then ask him to begin to restore your connection with him and to develop his nature in you.

THE GREATEST THREAT TO KINGDOM PRIVILEGES AND BENEFITS IS AN INDEPENDENT SPIRIT.

NOTES

Chapter Four

THE PROMISE OF THE GOVERNOR'S RETURN

CHAPTER THEME

Understanding the Creator-King's program to restore humanity puts the entire Old Testament in the proper light. It is not a group of stories strung together, a religious history, or a handbook of rituals. It is about the King initiating his plan to reestablish the Governor on earth and enable human beings to fulfill their original purpose and calling.

Questions for Reflection

1. Are the Old Testament and New Testament connected? In what way(s)?

2. Do you generally cooperate with the way God is working in your life, or do you resist it? Why?

Exploring Principles and Purposes

3. The restoration of the King's Spirit to humanity is central to the _____ _____ _____ _____ _____ _____. (p. 72)

4. What is the principal purpose of the redemptive program of the King in his dealings with humanity throughout human history? (p. 72)

5. While its events revolve around the people and nation of Israel, what is the universal theme of the Old Testament? (p. 73)

6. What implications would the restoration of the Spirit have regarding the purpose for which human beings were created? (p. 73)

7. All the situations, people, and programs in the Old Testament serve what five ends? (p. 74)

    (1)

    (2)

    (3)

    (4)

    (5)

8. When human beings lost the King's Spirit, they became unholy. What two meanings of holiness are emphasized in this chapter, and what do these concepts signify? (p. 75)

    (1)

    (2)

9. What does it mean for the Creator-King to be a "holy" God? (p. 76)

10. What does it mean for a human being to have personal holiness? (p. 76)

11. Why was the King's Spirit unable to return to the King's children? (pp. 76–77)

12. For the Governor to be restored to human beings, something had to happen to change their _____-_____ _____. (p. 77)

13. Briefly describe the three stages of the King's plan to fully restore the Governor to earth. (pp. 77–78)

    (1)

    (2)

    (3)

14. What is the identity of the Offspring who would come to earth, defeat Lucifer, reconcile the King's children to their Father, and restore the Governor? (p. 78)

15. Throughout the history of the Old Testament, the King-Father was preparing the earth to receive the _____-_____ (the Offspring). (p. 78)

16. From the events of Genesis 4 onward, the King-Father was working to set apart and preserve a _____ dedicated to his Son's eventual coming to earth. (p. 78)

17. What always accompanied the Governor's presence on earth through the submission of individuals to the heavenly government? (pp. 78–79)

18. What is the definition of a miracle, from the point of view of the heavenly kingdom? (p. 79)

19. What was the purpose of the worldwide flood, and why were Noah and his family preserved in the midst of it? (p. 79)

20. What do the King's words to Noah after the flood reveal about the King's purposes for humanity? (p. 79)

21. Abraham and Sarah cooperated with the King's plan, even though they did not fully understand it. They were given a child in their old age through the influence of the heavenly government in their lives. What major purposes of the King's plan would occur through the birth of their son, Isaac? (p. 80)

    (1)

    (2)

22. Noah and Abraham believed and obeyed the King's instructions. These were the means of their _____ or righteousness before him. (p. 80)

23. What does the word *righteousness* refer to? (p. 80)

24. Which of Isaac's twin sons was chosen to carry on the lineage of the Offspring? What did the King change his name to? (pp. 80–81)

25. What did Jacob's twelve sons become? Which of these sons was chosen to carry on the Offspring's lineage? (p. 81)

26. Why did the King preserve the Israelite nation through Moses and others? (p. 82)

27. What was the special calling of the Israelites in the King's plan? (pp. 82–83)

28. Describe the respective functions of "kingdom" and "priests." (p. 82)

29. The nation of Israel was to reflect the King's original plan for humanity, which was this: Every human being was created to be a _____—personally aligned with the Creator-King—and a _____—having dominion over the earth. (p. 82)

30. Why did the King give the law to the Israelites? (pp. 82–83, 85)

31. What would happen if the Israelites followed the law? (pp. 83, 85)

32. To what extend did the Israelites fulfill their purpose in the King's plan? (p. 83)

33. The King ultimately desired that his laws... [choose one] (p. 84)

    (a) be recorded on stone tablets

    (b) be recorded on paper

    (c) exist in the spirit of people's minds

    (d) be forced upon people's minds

34. Briefly describe the purpose of the priesthood, the sacrifices, and the rituals in Israel. (pp. 86–87)

35. All the temporary sacrifices brought the Governor into the people's _____, but not into _____. The sacrifices couldn't change their _____ nature. (pp. 87–88)

36. What did the Israelites' desire for a king reveal about them? (p. 90)

37. How did the Creator-King ultimately use the institution of kings in Israel to further his redemptive purposes? (p. 90)

38. What was the purpose of prophets in Israel? (pp. 91–92)

39. The Israelite people became perpetually unaligned with the King and were taken captive by Babylon, essentially ending the prototype nation. What was the next step in the King's plan to redeem humanity and fully restore the Governor to earth? (pp. 92–93)

40. How did the King communicate this extraordinary plan to the inhabitants of earth? (pp. 93–94)

41. The prophet Joel's message from the heavenly kingdom indicated... [choose one] (p. 95)

    (a) the King wants all people of the earth to receive the Governor.

    (b) the Governor will return to dwell in young and old, male and female.

    (c) the Governor will enable people to obey the King naturally.

    (d) all of the above

42. Why did Joel refer to the time of the Spirit's coming as "the day of the LORD" (Joel 2:11)? (p. 96)

43. In the New Testament, what did John the Baptist mean when he said, "The kingdom of heaven is near" (Matthew 3:2)? (p. 97)

44. John the Baptist said that when the King came to earth, he would "baptize [people] with the Holy Spirit and with fire" (Matthew 3:11). What would the King accomplish by this? (p. 97)

Conclusion

The Old Testament contains the repetition of the King's promise to return the Governor, as well as the evidence of heavenly kingdom influence selectively manifested through those who were submitted to the kingdom. Through his intervention in the lives of individuals and the prototype nation of Israel, the King announced that he himself was coming to earth as a human being to bring about this promised restoration.

Applying the Principles of Kingdom Living

Thinking It Over

• Has your perspective on the Old Testament changed through reading chapter four and doing this study? If so, in what ways?

• The King said through the prophet Jeremiah, "I will put my law in their minds and write it on their hearts. I will be their God, and they will be my people" (Jeremiah 31:33). Are you still trying to serve God in your own strength through rules and regulations that are not really a part of your nature? Or are you living by the nature of the King planted within your heart, through the power of his Spirit?

Acting on It

- Dr. Munroe defined personal holiness as being "one with yourself." If you are truly holy, you don't say something and then do something contrary to it. Your public behavior is the same as your private behavior. Think about your own life and list areas in which you need to become consistent in what you think, say, and do.

- In the "Questions for Reflection" section at the beginning of this study, you were asked whether you felt you were cooperating with the way God is working in your life, or resisting it. Write down any ways in which you are resisting his work in your life and make a conscious decision to yield to his purposes.

Praying about It

- Review the list you wrote concerning areas of personal holiness you need to work on. Ask God to help you become more consistent in these areas through the guidance and power of His Spirit.

- We learned through this study that God's purposes for humanity have not changed. He still desires that every human being function as a priest—continually aligned with him—and as a ruler—exercising dominion on the earth in his behalf through his Spirit. Ask God to enable you to fulfill these purposes in your life.

"I WILL POUR OUT MY SPIRIT ON ALL PEOPLE."
—JOEL 2:28

Part 2

THE RETURN OF THE GOVERNOR

Chapter Five

THE REBIRTH OF A KINGDOM

CHAPTER THEME

The heavenly King's mission on earth as a perfect human being was (1) to deliver the message and demonstrate the influence of the kingdom, and (2) to provide a way for rebellious humanity to be reconciled to the kingdom, receive the Spirit of the kingdom, and do the will of the kingdom on earth. The only way the holiness (internal integrity and devotion to the King) of human beings could be restored was through a sacrifice that paid the penalty of death for their rebellion.

Questions for Reflection

1. Have you made resolutions to obey God but continually failed to live up to them? If so, what do you think is the reason for this?

2. Is the kingdom of God a central focus of your life? How much of your thinking and lifestyle is influenced by the purposes of the kingdom?

Exploring Principles and Purposes

3. While the Old Testament emphasizes the _____ of the coming King, the New Testament reveals the _____ of the kingdom on earth through his _____. (p. 101)

4. The King needed to remain in the heavenly kingdom as its ruler. At the same time, he had to come to earth as the Offspring to provide for the return of the Governor. How was the Spirit of the King directly involved in the King's coming to earth as a human being? (p. 103)

5. In what way did the Governor return to earth when the King-Son was born? (p. 103)

6. As God the Son, the King-Son was fully _____. (p. 103)

7. As the man Jesus, the King-Son was fully _____. (p. 103)

8. How was the man Jesus different from other human beings? (p. 103)

9. How was Jesus like human beings before they rebelled? (p. 103)

10. What did John the Baptist say about the measure to which the Spirit of the King was in Jesus? What can we conclude by this? (pp. 104–105)

11. The Governor gave the _____-_____ to the earth so the King-Son could send the _____ to the earth after he returned to the _____ _____. (p. 104)

12. What three declarations did John make about Jesus when he came to him for baptism, and what do we learn from them? (p. 105)

    (1)

    (2)

    (3)

13. God the Father, God the Son, and God the Spirit are _____. The King expresses himself in _____ unique dimensions, which he revealed in his plan to restore humanity. (pp. 105–106)

14. God the Father is the _____, and Jesus Christ is the _____ who came in _____ _____. (p. 106)

15. What was the King-Son's mission on earth? (p. 106)

16. What was the purpose and nature of the kingdom the King-Son came to bring? (pp. 106–107)

    (1)

    (2)

17. What had the inhabitants of the colony of earth been doing to the King's territory? (p. 107)

18. What right did the King have to reclaim the earth? (p. 107)

19. How did the King-Son refer to Lucifer, and what did he intend to do to him? (p. 107)

20. Why did New Testament theologian Paul of Tarsus call Jesus the "last" or Second Adam? (p. 108)

21. Why can the kingdom of heaven be called a "family of kings"? (p. 108)

22. What was the central theme of Jesus' message throughout his three-and-a-half year ministry? (pp. 108–109)

23. You could say that the kingdom of heaven is the _____ where the King-Father resides, while the kingdom of God is the _____ of that country on its territories. (p. 109)

24. How and why did Lucifer try to tempt Jesus away from his mission? (p. 109–110)

25. How did Jesus overcome this temptation? (p. 110)

26. Jesus was tempted by Lucifer just after his baptism by John. What did Dr. Munroe say the act of baptism signified? (pp. 110–111)

27. The Greek word we translate as *disciple* means… [choose one] (p. 111)

    (a) discipline

    (b) pupil

    (c) slave

    (d) relative

28. To be a disciple was to join a philosopher or teacher's _____ _____ _____. (p. 111)

29. True or False: [circle one] (p. 112)

    A disciple was dedicated to more than one master teacher.

30. Why did the Creator-King choose to use the relationship of Master Teacher to disciples to reintroduce the kingdom to the world? (p. 112)

31. John the Baptist's message about the kingdom was… [choose one] (p. 113)

    (a) different from Jesus' message.

    (b) contradictory to Jesus' message.

    (c) the same as Jesus' message.

    (d) a slight variation of Jesus' message.

32. Why did Jesus, who was the ultimate Master Teacher, need to be baptized by John, a lesser master teacher? (p. 113)

33. What happened at Jesus' baptism confirming that the King-Father had appointed him Master Teacher of the kingdom school? (pp. 114–115)

34. What did the King-Father later say that also confirmed Jesus was the one to be listened to above all others? (p. 115)

35. When can we be considered followers of Jesus? (p. 115)

36. John the Baptist said Jesus would "baptize…with the Holy Spirit and with fire" (Matthew 3:11). What is the nature of the baptism with the Holy Spirit? (p. 116)

37. Why is a process of transformation into kingdom thinking and lifestyle absolutely necessary for the inhabitants of earth? (p. 116)

38. The _____ of the kingdom and the _____ and _____ of the Spirit are intimately connected. (p. 117)

39. What was Jesus' entire life on earth evidence of? (p. 117)

40. List some specific ways the administration of the kingdom of heaven was demonstrated in Jesus' life. (pp. 118–119)

41. Jesus said and did... [choose one] (pp. 118–119)

    (a) only what the King-Father initiated

    (b) only what he himself desired

    (c) what his disciples told him to do

    (d) what the crowds wanted

42. In addition to delivering the message and demonstrating the influence of the kingdom, Jesus' mission was to provide a way for the earth's inhabitants to be reconciled with the King and reenter the kingdom. What was the only way human beings' holiness could be restored? (p. 119)

43. What was the ultimate reason for the King's incarnation? (p. 119)

44. Why was Jesus able to be the ultimate sacrifice? (p. 120)

45. Jesus' death was… [choose one] (p. 120)

    (a) forced upon him.

    (b) an accident of fate.

    (c) a tragic mistake.

    (d) the result of his laying down his life voluntarily.

46. What authority did the King-Father give the King-Son in terms of his life? (p. 120)

47. What did this authority result in after the King-Son paid the penalty of death for the rebellion of humanity? (p. 120)

48. Paul described our entrance to the kingdom through the King-Son's sacrifice as walking in "_____ _____ _____." (p. 121)

49. What was the result of Jesus' completing the work of restoration for humanity? (p. 122)

50. Jesus' death and resurrection broke the spirit of _____ in humanity. He provided for this spirit to be replaced with a spirit of _____ to the kingdom. He gave us the ability to _____ the will of the Father. (p. 123)

51. Though Jesus paid the penalty for the rebellion of all humanity, what is the responsibility of each person in receiving the results of Jesus' sacrifice? (p. 125)

52. Jesus' sacrificial death and resurrection not only meant reconciliation between the King and the inhabitants of earth. It also meant the Governor could now take up official residence again in the _____ of the kingdom on _____. (p. 125)

53. What is the Holy Spirit the source of in our lives? (p. 127)

54. The Holy Spirit is the heavenly government _____. (p. 127)

55. For a kingdom citizen empowered by the King's Spirit, what is the essential meaning of this phrase in the Lord's Prayer: "Our Father in heaven, hallowed be your name, *your kingdom come, your will be done on earth as it is in heaven*" (Matthew 6:9–10, emphasis added)? (p. 128)

56. The Governor would _____ the earth once more into a _____ of heaven through the return of the _____ in the lives of its citizens. (p. 131)

Conclusion

The King-Son gave up his life in sacrifice so human beings could be cleansed vessels for the Governor to live in. His death on the cross, the blood that he shed, and his resurrection from the dead were required in order to break the spirit of rebellion in humanity, which is antagonistic to the kingdom of heaven. When Jesus broke the spirit of rebellion, this allowed the earth's inhabitants to yield to the Holy Spirit and the purposes of the kingdom. At Jesus' resurrection, therefore, the Spirit was poised to return to humanity and rescue those living in rebellion, confusion, and despair under the kingdom of darkness.

Applying the Principles of Kingdom Living

Thinking It Over

• Have you made a solid decision to be a disciple in Jesus' kingdom school, so that you *know* you have forever chosen him above all other possible teachers and philosophies on earth? Why or why not?

• It is essential to remember and be thankful for the sacrifice Jesus made on the cross to enable us to be restored to the Father. Yet have you moved beyond a contemplation of Christ's ultimate sacrifice and entered into the reason for which he made it? Have you allowed the Holy Spirit to fill your life so you are living according to the mind and heart of God and in the power of his Spirit?

Acting on It

- Dr. Munroe reminded us that the word *repentance* does not specifically refer to emotions and crying, but it means "to change your mind, to reverse your way of thinking and acting." Has this been your attitude concerning areas in your life that are not in alignment with the kingdom of God? Write about how you would think and act differently in your life, based on true repentance.

- As a student enrolled in Jesus' kingdom school, read a portion of Jesus' words or actions from one of the four Gospels every day. Then apply its teaching, wisdom, or directives to your own life.

Praying about It

- Make this the prayer of your heart every day to the King-Father: "Our Father in heaven, hallowed be your name, your kingdom come, your will be done on earth as it is in heaven" (Matthew 6:9–10).

THE ONLY WAY TO LIVE THE LIFE OF THE KINGDOM IS TO BE SUBMERGED IN THE MIND-SET OF THE KING.

NOTES

Chapter Six

A King's Love for His Citizens

Chapter Theme

Sacrificial love is the nature of the King and his kingdom. When the King-Son came to earth, he revealed the nature of the King-Father to human beings who no longer knew their God and were trapped in a kingdom of darkness under Lucifer. The King didn't want the earth's inhabitants to experience spiritual death as a result of their rebellion, and therefore he willingly died in our place. Jesus took away our fear of God by reconciling us to him through his sacrifice, and giving us the gift of his Spirit. In doing so, he enabled us to call God not only our King, but also our Father again, because we have the same Spirit within us.

Questions for Reflection

1. Do you tend to feel assured and confident in your relationship with God or fearful of him? Why?

2. How would you describe God's character?

3. Do you usually think of Jesus as just like God or as being somewhat different from God? In what ways?

Exploring Principles and Purposes

4. The King-Son's motivation for coming to earth was _____ _____ for its inhabitants. (p. 133)

5. What did the King-Son choose to do as a result of this motivation? (p. 133)

6. Jesus is the perfect _____ of God in human form. (p. 133)

7. What is the essential nature of the King-Father and the King-Son? (p. 133)

8. In what four ways did the King-Son limit himself so he could send the Governor back to us—and *in* us—without limitations? (pp. 134–135)

   (1)

   (2)

   (3)

   (4)

9. How did the King-Son limit himself from glory? (pp. 135–136)

10. How did the King-Son limit himself to time and space? (pp. 136–137)

11. How did the King-Son limit himself under law? (p. 137)

12. How did the King-Son limit himself by death? (p. 138)

13. What did the King-Son do that is virtually unheard of in our experience of human leaders? (p. 139)

14. In what way did the King-Son's limitation of death and subsequent resurrection bring unlimited life for us? (p. 138)

15. How did the King-Son's absence from the earth, when he returned to the King-Father after his resurrection, bring unlimited kingdom influence to the earth? (pp. 139–141)

16. Where would we be if the King-Son had not died for us and been resurrected? (p. 141)

17. Where would we be if the King-Son had not returned to the heavenly home country and sent the Governor to us? (p. 141)

18. How did the King-Father feel about restoring the kingdom to human beings again through the Holy Spirit? (p. 142)

19. The Holy Spirit is a _____ gift to humanity. (p. 142)

Conclusion

Jesus limited himself in the many ways that he did as a human being on earth out of deep self-sacrificial love and devotion to the estranged children of the King. He made restoration possible for all the inhabitants of the world and brought unlimited kingdom influence to earth through the Governor's presence in the lives of kingdom citizens everywhere.

Applying the Principles of Kingdom Living

Thinking It Over

• What have you learned from this study about the nature of the God the Father and God the Son?

• Describe God's attitude toward you. Has your perspective on this changed at all since reading chapter six and doing this study? If so, in what ways?

Acting on It

• Do you often feel things would be better for you if Jesus was living on earth today? In what ways is your life better with Jesus in heaven and the Holy Spirit living within you?

- Jesus provided unlimited kingdom influence for the world through the gift of the Holy Spirit in the lives of kingdom citizens. What do you think you are meant to do with this gift? Record some of your ideas, below.

Praying about It

- Thank your heavenly Father for the priceless gift of the Holy Spirit in your life, and ask the Father to use you to spread his kingdom influence in the world.

- Do you struggle with accepting God's unqualified love for you? Ask him to enable you to both understand and receive his love, so you may live in the sure knowledge of it as you help spread the message of the kingdom through his Spirit.

LOVE IS THE NATURE OF THE KING AND HIS KINGDOM.

NOTES

Chapter Seven

RESTORING THE CONNECTION

CHAPTER THEME

After Jesus' resurrection, the work of preparing humanity to receive the Holy Spirit was complete. The spirit of rebellion and independence from the kingdom was broken. Any human being who personally receives the sacrifice of the King-Son, applying it to his own life, is cleansed and qualified to be a residence for the Governor. Jesus promised his disciples concerning the Holy Spirit, "He lives with you and will be in you" (John 14:17). He would reconnect them to the Father through the Spirit, and they would receive the presence and power of the kingdom.

Questions for Reflection

1. Do you often find you have the desire but not the ability to spread God's kingdom in the world? What do you think might be hindering you?

2. What are some distinguishing characteristics of the kingdom of heaven?

Exploring Principles and Purposes

3. Jesus' life, ministry, death, and resurrection led up to his most important act on earth: _____ _____ ____ _____ _____. (p. 143).

4. How was the Holy Spirit initially given to Jesus' disciples? (p. 143)

5. How was this giving of the Spirit similar to another momentous event in human history? (p. 144)

6. What did Jesus indicate by the words he used when he gave the Spirit to his disciples? (p. 144)

7. In giving the Spirit, Jesus was restoring to human beings what they had _____. (p. 144)

8. What did this initial giving of the Spirit to Jesus' disciples signify? (pp. 144–145)

9. True or False: [circle one] (p. 145)

   Jesus' central message after his resurrection was different from his message before his resurrection.

   Explain your answer.

10. How do we know the kingdom of heaven is on earth right now? (pp. 145–146)

11. Even though Jesus had already breathed the Spirit on his disciples and they had received the Governor in their lives and been reconnected to the kingdom, what did they still need to be connected to? (p. 147)

12. What statement had John the Baptist made about Jesus that related to this connection? (p. 147)

13. Write down two statements Jesus made about the disciples receiving power through the Holy Spirit. (p. 147)

    (1)

    (2)

14. What is significant about the disciples receiving the power of the Governor from "on high"? (p. 148)

15. Describe how the Governor was poured out on Jesus' followers after he ascended to heaven—"on high." (p. 148)

16. Why were Jesus' followers given the ability to speak in other languages after they were filled with the Holy Spirit? (pp. 148–149)

17. What were these languages an evidence of? (p. 149)

18. The King-Father had promised—at the time of humanity's rebellion, numerous times throughout the Old Testament, and through the ministries of John the Baptist and the King-Son—that the Governor would return. This promise was now _____. (pp. 149–150)

19. Peter told the crowds at Pentecost they were witnessing the _____ of the _____ of heaven through the arrival of the Governor. (p. 150)

20. What separates the kingdom of heaven from all other philosophies, belief systems, and religions? (p. 150)

21. Jesus' purpose is to spread the kingdom of God on earth through a multitude of _____, in a multitude of _____, in all _____ of _____. (p. 150)

22. Why does the King want us to represent his kingdom on earth? (p. 151)

23. What is the meaning of Jesus' statement, "I tell you the truth, anyone who has faith in me will do what I have been doing. He will do *even greater things* than these, because I am going to the Father" (John 14:12, emphasis added)? (p. 151)

24. The power of the Governor is that he makes the _____ of heaven on earth _____. (p. 152)

25. Why is the Governor the most important person on earth? (p. 152)

Conclusion

The return of the Holy Spirit was the most important act of redemption in God's program for humanity. With the giving of the Spirit, the kingdom of God returned to earth because the Spirit lived within humanity once more. Through the Governor, human beings could be restored to their standing as vice governors in the kingdom. They could also receive the power of the kingdom of heaven to work its purposes in the world and drive out the kingdom of darkness. The citizens of the kingdom would multiply the influence of the heavenly government throughout the world, bringing glory to God the Father and God the Son and making heaven on earth a reality.

Applying the Principles of Kingdom Living

Thinking It Over

- Do you exhibit clear evidence of the influence of the heavenly government in your life?

Acting on It

- If the Spirit lives within you, then the influence of the heavenly government is present wherever you are. Write how you can bring the influence of the heavenly government to…

Your home (family)?

Your workplace?

Your school?

Your friends?

People you meet at stores, restaurants, appointments?

Your church?

Praying about It

- Ask your heavenly Father to help you exhibit the influence of his kingdom wherever you go.

- Pray for someone specifically this week who needs to be reconciled to the King-Father and enter the kingdom of heaven.

**"THE KINGDOM OF GOD IS WITHIN YOU."
—LUKE 17:21**

Chapter Eight

REINSTATING THE GOVERNOR

CHAPTER THEME

Our entrance into the kingdom of heaven, also called the "new birth," results in the restoration of our legal authority as rulers on earth. Then, our baptism in the Holy Spirit results in the restoration of our power or ability to carry out that authority. Having a better understanding of these two concepts will enable us to be effective as we live out the culture of the kingdom on earth, for both have to do with the reinstatement of the Governor to his place and role in our lives.

Questions for Reflection

1. Do you generally feel connected or disconnected from God? Explain why you feel this way.

2. How would you present the claims of the kingdom of God to someone of another culture?

Exploring Principles and Purposes

3. After entering into the kingdom of heaven, or the new birth, how can we be constantly connected to the life of the kingdom? (p. 154)

4. The new birth _____ human beings to the _____ of heaven. (p. 154)

5. What did Paul mean when he referred to the Holy Spirit as a "deposit" in our lives? (p. 154)

6. The new birth _____ human beings to full _____ in the heavenly realm. (p. 155)

7. The new birth _____ the _____ on earth through humanity. (p. 155)

8. The more inhabitants of earth who enter the kingdom of heaven… [choose one] (p. 155)

    (a) the less they are needed on earth

    (b) the more the kingdom influence should be felt on earth

    (c) the less the kingdom influence is felt on earth

    (d) the more others are needed to replace them

9. The new birth restores inter-realm _____ and _____ to the unseen world. (p. 155)

10. We not only have _____ to the unseen world, but we also have _____ there as we pursue the purposes of the kingdom. (p. 156)

11. The new birth restores the _____ of the _____ within humanity (p. 156)

12. The new birth prepares us for restored relationship with the Father. What does the baptism in the Holy Spirit prepare us for? (p. 157)

13. While the new birth is described as a well of water springing up, what is the baptism in the Holy Spirit described as? What is the significance of this word picture to heavenly influence on earth? (p. 158)

14. The baptism in the Holy Spirit restores the power of _____. (p. 158)

15. What is the definition of power? (p. 158)

16. The baptism in the Holy Spirit restores humanity's ability to _____ the _____. (p. 158)

17. What enables kingdom citizens to give evidence of the presence, authority, and power of the government of God on earth? (p. 159)

18. The baptism in the Holy Spirit enables human beings to _____ the claims of the King. (p. 160)

19. The baptism in the Holy Spirit gives human beings the ability to _____ the _____ of the King and his kingdom. (p. 160)

20. The works that kingdom citizens do through the power of the Governor... [choose one] (p. 160)

    (a) will never be understood by other people

    (b) could be understood only in the first-century

    (c) are limited to certain languages and cultures

    (d) transcend human language and culture

21. The baptism in the Holy Spirit gives human beings the ability to _____ heavenly _____. (p. 161)

22. How can the baptism be compared to a passport? (p. 161)

23. Who is the one who can exercise the power of the heavenly kingdom? (pp. 161–162)

24. Who respected and obeyed Paul's authority as an authorized citizen of heaven? (p. 162)

25. What steps did Dr. Munroe present, based on Peter's instructions to the crowds at Pentecost, for being reconciled to the King-Father and receiving the Governor? (pp. 162–163)

(1)

(2)

26. What is the kingdom life? (p. 164)

Conclusion

Both the new birth and the baptism in the Holy Spirit are necessary for living the kingdom life. Without the new birth, we do not have the relationship with and the authority of the King to carry out his purposes on earth. Without the baptism in the Holy Spirit, we can still have good intentions of fulfilling the work of the kingdom. However, we will be frustrated because we will not have the power to do so. Our King has given us all the resources we need to be his representatives on earth. He desires that we receive the kingdom authority and power he has sacrificed to give us.

Applying the Principles of Kingdom Living

Thinking It Over

• Do you have both a relationship with God *and* the power through the Holy Spirit to fulfill his purposes on earth? Why or why not?

• Are you trusting in God to supply all your needs in life as you pursue the purposes of the kingdom? If not, what prevents you from doing this?

Acting on It

- Have you taken the first step to be reconnected to your heavenly Father? If you haven't, decide today to repent (desire to live according to the kingdom) and receive the forgiveness provided through Jesus' sacrifice. Then, accept the gift of the Holy Spirit and thank God for sending him to live within you.

- Are you seeking the kingdom first in your life? What areas do you need to dedicate to kingdom purposes?

- Have you been baptized in water as a sign that you have joined the kingdom school, with Jesus as your Master Teacher? Why not take this public step of identification and alignment with the kingdom?

Praying about It

- Dr. Munroe wrote that, with the new birth, there is a continuous reservoir of God's Spirit within us, much like a spring forever bubbling up with fresh, clean, life-giving water. As we continually drink deeply from this water of the Spirit within us, we will constantly be connected to the life of the kingdom. If you are feeling spiritually dry, ask God to enable you to "drink deeply of this water" by drawing on the love and power of the Spirit, who dwells within you.

- Paul wrote in Ephesians 5:1–2, "Be imitators of God, therefore, as dearly loved children and live a life of love, just as Christ loved us and gave himself up for us as a fragrant offering and sacrifice to God." Ask your heavenly Father to enable you to be an imitator of him by reflecting his nature in the world.

THE NEW BIRTH PREPARES US FOR HEAVEN. THE BAPTISM IN THE SPIRIT PREPARES US FOR EARTH.

NOTES

Chapter Nine

RESULTS OF RECONNECTION

CHAPTER THEME

Without the Governor, a person cannot be a citizen of the heavenly kingdom. Just as DNA pinpoints the identity of a person, the Spirit of God within a person identifies him as a kingdom citizen. There is no margin of error. When you are connected to the King through his Governor, an entirely new and remarkable life opens up for you. This new life reflects the many results of reconnection associated with a fully authorized citizen of the realm.

Question for Reflection

1. How has your outlook on life changed since you became a kingdom citizen? Are there any areas that have stayed the same that you think should better reflect the mind-set of the kingdom?

Exploring Principles and Purposes

2. What is the first result of reconnection with the heavenly kingdom? (p. 166)

3. When the Governor enters a person's life, he connects that person to his _____ of life, and with all the _____ and _____ of a member of the heavenly royal family. (p. 166)

4. What two things must we acknowledge of our King-Father as we are reconnected to him? (p. 166)

   (1)

   (2)

5. What is the second result of reconnection with the heavenly kingdom? (p. 166)

6. The coming of the Governor affirmed the access to the kingdom, and the value to the kingdom, of what types of people who will receive the Spirit? (pp. 166–170)

7. All human beings lost the Holy Spirit when humanity rebelled, but God desires _____ to be reconciled to him and to be _____ with the Governor. (p. 170)

8. Receiving the Holy Spirit into your life makes you… [choose one] (p. 170)

   (a) better than other people

   (b) able to hoard the knowledge of the kingdom for yourself

   (c) a steward of kingdom authority and power

   (d) not responsible for telling others about the kingdom message

9. What is the third result of reconnection? (p. 170)

10. What are the two kinds of kingdom authority, and how are they defined? (p. 171)

    (1)

    (2)

11. True or False: [circle one] (p. 172)

    If you have delegated-authority but not ability-authority, you will still see much accomplished.

12. Through the baptism in the Holy Spirit, kingdom citizens have all the _____ of _____ (ability-authority) to carry out their assignment. (p. 173)

13. Dr. Munroe explained that the authority of a royal governor was in the name of the sovereign of the country he was serving. His own name had no real weight. He used the King's name to exercise authority in getting things done. How does our influence and authority as kingdom citizens under the Governor function in a similar way? (pp. 173–174)

14. What statement did Jesus make to his followers showing that the Governor would confirm their authority as legal agents of the kingdom by backing them up with the power of the heavenly government? (p. 175)

15. God's *original* and *eternal* assignment for humanity is _____ _____ on earth for the kingdom of God. (p. 176)

16. What did the King-Father promise would happen when Lucifer and the kingdom of darkness are totally defeated? (p. 176)

17. What is the fourth result of reconnection? (p. 177)

18. It is impossible to really be in the kingdom of God and not experience _____. (p. 177)

19. With a transformed outlook, there is a realignment of the proper functioning of a person's _____, _____, and _____. (p. 177)

20. In the critical conflict between the mind-set of the kingdom of heaven and the mind-set of the kingdom of darkness, how can our outlook be transformed? (p. 178)

21. We need to change our _____-_____ if we are to have the same _____ of the King in order to help rule the earth. (p. 178)

22. What is the fifth result of reconnection? (p. 180)

23. What truths about the King and his government are the basis for this result? (p. 180)

24. Why is the fear of man a snare to kingdom citizens? (p. 181)

25. Paul wrote that the King has not given us the spirit of fear but of _____, _____, and a _____ _____. (p. 181) [See 2 Timothy 1:7 NKJV.]

26. What is the sixth result of reconnection? (p. 181)

27. How did Dr. Munroe define a dream? A vision? (p. 181)

    Dream:

    Vision:

28. When did the King plan for us to accomplish specific good works for his kingdom? (p. 181)

29. The King makes us all rulers in the _____ of our particular _____. (p. 182)

30. True or False: [circle one] (p. 182)

    The Governor came to give you a vision or a dream that only you can help accomplish, as well as the power to accomplish it, as your special work on earth.

31. What is the seventh result of reconnection? (p. 182)

32. What do we need if we are going to bring the kingdom of heaven to earth and have dominion? (p. 182)

33. What two avenues give us complete access to the Father and enable us to know his will for us? (pp. 183–184)

(1)

(2)

34. List several aspects of the nature of worship in relation to the King-Father and the outworking of his government on earth. (pp. 185–186)

Conclusion

Many wonderful and essential benefits occur when a person is reconnected to the kingdom of heaven through the indwelling Holy Spirit. Many of these benefits must be clearly recognized and acted upon if we are to enter into the fullness of our standing as beloved children and authorized citizens of the realm. When we do understand them and act on them in faith, we will see the influence of the kingdom actively working in our lives and the lives of those around us.

Applying the Principles of Kingdom Living

Thinking It Over

- Jesus said, "All authority in heaven and on earth has been given to me. Therefore go and make disciples of all nations" (Matthew 28:18–19), and "You will receive power when the Holy Spirit comes on you" (Acts 1:8). How much have you thought about the authority you have been given to carry out the work of the kingdom—that you have both delegated-authority and ability-authority? How would a true understanding of these types of authority in your life change the way you live and interact with others?

- We have seen that whenever a communication of the Governor is *ignored* by a kingdom citizen, the practical rulership of the King is absent on earth. In what ways might you be ignoring the clear communication of the Holy Spirit regarding kingdom purposes? How can you restore the practical rulership of the King in your life?

Acting on It

Paul wrote, "Do not conform any longer to the pattern of this world, but be transformed by the renewing of your mind. Then you will be able to test and approve what God's will is—his good, pleasing and perfect will" (Romans 12:2), and "Live by the Spirit, and you will not gratify the desires of the sinful nature" (Galatians 5:16). When we become kingdom citizens, our minds are to be transformed so we will no longer have a mind-set filled with rebellion, guilt, depression, fear, confusion, and frustration, but rather one that reflects the nature of the kingdom—righteousness, peace, and joy in the Holy Spirit.

• What steps are you taking to renew your mind according to the nature of the kingdom? Regularly reading the Scriptures—the Constitution of the kingdom—enables us to learn the King's will and "take captive every thought to make it obedient to Christ" (2 Corinthians 10:5). Write what you are doing and would like to do in renewing your mind:

• Another way to renew our minds is to take on the history of the kingdom rather than allowing our past sins and failings to defeat us. Our history as the human race and as individuals is one of rebellion, fallenness, distorted and lost purpose, and death. But when we are born anew into the kingdom of heaven, we have a history of redemption, forgiveness, love, hope, vision, and life. Our sins are blotted out, and God does not remember them any longer. We now have purpose and potential. Which history are you choosing for yourself? How will you take on the history of the kingdom in your life?

Praying about It

• Dr. Munroe said the King-Father gives us visions of what we can accomplish in our lifetimes, and dreams of what we can see being accomplished in the future, even though we may not live to see them fully completed. What vision or dream do you have? Ask the Father to clarify this for you and show you how to fulfill his purposes for your life. Allow the Governor to empower you to impact the earth for heaven through *your* vision or dream.

"IF YOU REMAIN IN ME AND MY WORDS REMAIN IN YOU, ASK WHATEVER YOU WISH, AND IT WILL BE GIVEN YOU."
—JOHN 15:7

Part 3

UNDERSTANDING THE GOVERNOR

Chapter Ten

THE NATURE OF THE GOVERNOR

CHAPTER THEME

People who are not yet in the kingdom do not understand the Holy Spirit's indispensable role in their lives because they have been led to believe he is mysterious and unknowable. Or they think he is a kind of apparition because of our modern connotation of the word *spirit* and the use of the term *Holy Ghost* for Holy Spirit in the King James Version of the Bible. Even people who have received the Governor have misconceptions regarding who he is. Some think he is a sensation or a thrill whose purpose is to make them "feel good." It is therefore essential for us to understand the Governor's true nature. The Holy Spirit is divine, he is a person, and he has many attributes that enable us to fulfill our calling as citizens of the heavenly kingdom.

Question for Reflection

1. What is your conception of the Holy Spirit's nature and qualities? What did you think the Holy Spirit was like when you were growing up or when you first became a Christian?

Exploring Principles and Purposes

2. Though the Governor is the most important person on earth, he is also the most
   _____ and _____ . (p. 189)

3. The Holy Spirit is... [choose one] (pp. 190–191)

    (a) a nonpersonal object or "thing"

    (b) smoke, cloud, or ethereal mist

    (c) a feeling or sensation

    (d) a distinct person with a personality

4. Even though the Holy Spirit is not a feeling, his presence can affect our
    _____ as we experience his peace, joy, and comfort. (p. 192)

5. The most important thing we must know about the nature of the Holy Spirit is that he
    is _____. (p. 192) He is _____ to the Father and the Son. (p. 193)

6. What did Dr. Munroe mean when he said the Holy Spirit is "God extended"? (p. 192)

7. God is one, but he expresses himself in three distinct _____ and
    _____. (p. 193)

8. Jesus said that blasphemy against the Holy Spirit is the only sin that cannot be forgiven.
    (See, for example, Mark 3:29.) What did Dr. Munroe say is the nature of this sin? (p.
    194)

9. What identifies the Holy Spirit as a person? (pp. 195–196)

10. In what way does the Holy Spirit have "senses" that are part of his personality? (p.
    196)

11. How do we know that the Holy Spirit has feelings or emotions? (p. 196)

12. When we neglect or ignore the Holy Spirit, what will he sometimes do in order to get our attention? (p. 197)

13. How can we learn to have fellowship with and listen to the Holy Spirit? (p. 198)

14. As we have seen, in his various roles and responsibilities on earth, the Governor acts only according to the _____ of the _____. (p. 198) [See John 16:13–15.]

15. There are seven distinct ways in which the Governor attends to us in fulfillment of his nature. What is the first of his roles and responsibilities toward us? (p. 198)

16. What is the literal definition of the Greek word translated as *Counselor* in John 14:16, 26? (pp. 198–199)

17. What analogy did Jesus use to emphasize the King's commitment to us, which also lets us know the Holy Spirit will never give up on us? (p. 199)

18. What is the second of the Holy Spirit's roles and responsibilities toward us? (p. 200)

19. Why is the Governor our most important teacher? (pp. 200–201)

20. How does the Governor make us practical people in the world? (p. 201)

21. What is the third of the Holy Spirit's roles and responsibilities toward us? (p. 201)

22. What is the first arena in which this help is given, and what does it involve? (p. 202)

23. What is the second arena in which this help is given, and what does it refer to? (p. 203)

24. No one's intellect alone can _____ or _____ the gifts the King has placed within him for the purposes of the _____. If you want to know what the Spirit of God really _____ inside you, you have to connect to the Governor. (p. 203)

25. Knowing the gifts God has given us through the Holy Spirit is vital for fulfilling our _____ and _____. (p. 204)

26. Name the two kinds of gifts we receive from God. (p. 204)

    (1)

    (2)

27. Which of these kinds of gifts is highlighted in this chapter? (p. 204)

28. In what way does the Holy Spirit empower us to use these particular gifts? (p. 204)

29. What is the fourth of the Holy Spirit's roles and responsibilities toward us? (p. 205)

30. How does the Holy Spirit exercise this role with those outside the kingdom of heaven? (p. 205)

31. How does the Holy Spirit exercise this role with those who have already entered the kingdom of heaven? (p. 205)

32. The Holy Spirit _____ us, but he never forces us. The King-Father respects our wills, and he wants his children to _____ what he _____. (p. 205)

33. What is the fifth of the Holy Spirit's roles and responsibilities toward us? (p. 206)

34. In what manner does the Holy Spirit fulfill this role, and what Scripture from Hosea illustrates it? (p. 206)

35. What is the sixth of the Holy Spirit's roles and responsibilities toward us? (p. 206)

36. What is the nature and content of the words or messages the Governor brings us? (p. 207)

37. What is the seventh of the Holy Spirit's roles and responsibilities toward us? (p. 207)

38. There are two main ways the Holy Spirit fulfills this role. What is the first one? (p. 207)

39. What is the second way the Holy Spirit fulfills this role? (pp. 207–208)

Conclusion

The Holy Spirit is God "extended" to us. He is a distinct person of the triune God who comes to us with love, encouragement, wisdom, and strength to work the purposes of the kingdom in our lives in a multitude of ways. He truly is the one who comes alongside us to assist us in fulfilling our particular roles and assignments as we help spread the kingdom on earth. His work in our lives is indispensable.

Applying the Principles of Kingdom Living

Thinking It Over

- Dr. Munroe wrote, "Most citizens of the kingdom have no real relationship with the Governor because they haven't realized they have someone invaluable dwelling in them." Have you thought of the Holy Spirit as an impersonal object, a feeling, or a force? Have you realized *who* you have living within you? How does this knowledge change the way you think of the Holy Spirit, and how will it change your relationship with him?

- Have you hesitated to make a commitment to the kingdom because you think you have to overcome sin and wrong attitudes *first*? Or have you struggled, even as a kingdom citizen, because you're trying to change your false mind-sets and behavior on your own? Remember that the King is saying to us, "If you're going to learn kingdom culture, you need help from the home country." Receiving the Governor first into your life will enable you to change. Recognize that he will show you how to transform your thinking and how to live for the kingdom. The King sent him to us for this very purpose.

Acting on It

- Has the Holy Spirit been prompting you that it is time to repent, seek forgiveness, and enter the kingdom of God? Have you been resisting that prompting? Run to him now! As one of the New Testament writers reminded us, "Today, if you hear his voice, do not harden your hearts as you did in the rebellion" (Hebrews 3:15). God is long-suffering (patient), but he is not forever-suffering. We must respond to him when he calls us or it may become too late to respond.

- Take each of the roles and responsibilities of the Holy Spirit we have explored in this chapter and meditate on them until you come to a thorough understanding of the way the Governor works in your life. You may want to focus on one per day, week, or month. Search the Scriptures for evidence of his working in these ways in the lives of people in the first century. Ask the Governor to reveal his nature to you, and yield to his promptings and desire to help you in your kingdom life.

Praying about It

- Dr. Munroe taught that the Holy Spirit is a person who knows when we are ignoring him. If we disregard his teaching and leading, we aren't treating him with the respect and devotion he deserves. We also miss opportunities to learn and serve others for the kingdom. Do you seek the advice of people without ever consulting your Teacher and Guide? Do you go through your day without acknowledging him or referring to him as you make decisions, invest your finances, work at your job or business, or go to school? Make a decision to acknowledge and inquire of the Holy Spirit every morning and throughout the day. This will help you to build a relationship with him, learn to hear his voice, and fulfill the will of God in your life.

THE HOLY SPIRIT'S PRESENCE IN OUR LIVES IS INDISPENSABLE.

NOTES

Chapter Eleven

THE GOVERNOR'S CULTURE

CHAPTER THEME

As kingdom citizens, we must always keep in mind that the culture of the kingdom of heaven is synonymous with the nature of the King. When we talk about the characteristics of the Holy Spirit and his culture, therefore, we are talking about the qualities of the King himself. As vice governors under the Royal Governor, we serve as ambassadors of this kingdom culture and are to reflect the King's nature in every area of our lives.

Question for Reflection

1. How have you seen the environment of an organization, school, business, family, or nation influenced (either positively or negatively) by the character of its leaders?

Exploring Principles and Purposes

2. A country's culture may be summed up as its national character. How is national character defined? (p. 210)

3. Why were a monarch's character and characteristics vastly important to his kingdom? (p. 210)

4. What is the key to a successful kingdom? (p. 212)

5. The _____ of the heavenly Governor determines the _____ of the kingdom of God on earth. His character is exactly the same as the character of the _____. (p. 212)

6. Why does the King-Father want us to understand the nature of his kingdom? (p. 212)

7. What notable statement about rulers did Jesus make to his disciples that shows the kingdom of heaven is radically different from the kingdom of darkness—and earthly kingdoms that are influenced by it? (p. 213) How would you define the central theme of this statement?

8. What essential qualities did Paul list as the nature of the heavenly King and his kingdom? (p. 214)

9. Wherever the Governor of the kingdom is, these qualities will be _____, indicating the culture of the King is _____. (p. 214)

10. Why did Paul use the particular analogy of fruit in describing the nature of the kingdom? (p. 214)

11. When you receive the Holy Spirit, you also receive the seed of kingdom nature. How do you develop this seed in your life? (pp. 214–215)

12. The fruit of the Spirit becomes a _____ development in the life of a kingdom citizen because he is reflecting the _____ of his King. (p. 215)

13. Explain the statement "Your culture should reveal your origin" in terms of the kingdom of heaven. (p. 216)

14. If the Governor lives in you, then living in rebellion against the King is... [choose one] (p. 216)

    (a) uncomfortable and unnatural

    (b) enjoyable

    (c) acceptable

    (d) natural

15. When you become realigned with the kingdom of heaven, what two worlds or kingdoms do you now live in? (pp. 216–217)

16. We are continually faced with the choice of which of these kingdoms and its culture we will yield to. What instruction do we find in the New Testament to help us remain aligned with the kingdom of heaven? (p. 217)

17. True or False: [circle one] (p. 219)

    The culture of heaven and the culture of the world are compatible; you can still experience the kingdom of heaven if you are living according to a foreign culture.

18. How does the Governor rebuke and correct us when we act according to the culture of darkness? (p. 219)

19. Trying to follow strict *dos* and *don't*s for our behavior doesn't work. Only a _____ nature causes us to live as the King lives. The Governor gives us this new nature and enables us to _____ it. (p. 219)

20. What challenging job does the Governor have? (p. 220)

21. What is the first thing the Governor teaches us? Why? (p. 220)

22. The qualities or fruit of the Spirit are not only what the King _____; they are what he _____. And every aspect of the King's nature is what we are to be in our _____, as well. (p. 220)

23. Realizing that we are to reflect the nature of our King-Father, what should we carefully watch in our lives? (pp. 220–221)

24. Since we ourselves are the Governor's _____ on earth, we need to keep his residence _____ for him. (p. 221)

25. What is a necessary experience for a kingdom citizen who lives in the middle of a culture of rebellion and death? (p. 221)

26. What is our purpose for being on earth while it is still influenced by the kingdom of darkness? (p. 221)

27. What reality do we live in at the same time we experience intercultural (inter-kingdom) tension? (p. 222)

28. The fruit of the Spirit has to do with the _____ of the King, and the gifts of the Spirit have to do with the _____ of the King. (p. 223)

29. In what different ways are the fruit and the gifts manifested in our lives? (p. 223)

30. While the fruit and the gifts are both essential for kingdom living, why is character more important than power? What is power without character? (p. 223)

31. Being transformed into the culture of the kingdom is an _____, _____ process. (p. 224)

32. Culture is spread through _____, and the qualities (fruit) and gifts of the Spirit are the _____ of the _____ on earth. (p. 224)

Conclusion

We have to be trained in what it means to be heirs in the heavenly kingdom. The Governor is like a royal tutor, instilling the nature of the kingdom into the King's children. In this way, we can effectively serve as ambassadors of kingdom culture under the Royal Governor. As we allow the Governor to transform our lives into the nature of the King, and as we demonstrate his power, our lives will have an effect on others. This is how the kingdom of heaven will spread on the earth. Kingdom influence will grow from personal commitment to community transformation to national impact to worldwide conversion.

Applying the Principles of Kingdom Living

Thinking It Over

- Are you living out the culture of the kingdom according to the fruit of the Spirit, so that people clearly recognize you as a citizen of the kingdom of heaven? Your culture should reveal your origin. The way you behave, the way you respond to others, the way you react to problems, and the way you deal with disappointments should all reveal the culture of heaven. What aspects of the fruit do you most need to develop, with the guidance and help of the Governor?

- Have you experienced a kingdom "culture clash" with members of your family, friends, or others who have not yet entered the kingdom of heaven? How have you responded to it? Have you asked the Governor to help you to respond according to the nature of the King?

Acting on It

• Dr. Munroe wrote that sometimes we try to have one foot in the kingdom of heaven and one foot in the kingdom of the world. We want the Governor to look the other way while we behave according to a culture that is foreign to the King's. Yet we have seen that the culture of the kingdom of heaven and the culture of the kingdom of darkness are totally incompatible. The kingdom of darkness can never reflect the nature of the King. In what areas of your life are you attempting to live in both kingdoms? Note these areas, surrender them to the Governor, and commit yourself to him for transformation into the nature of the King.

• Are you watching what you are allowing into the personal culture of your spirit, soul, and body? Whatever we keep listening to or watching inevitably influences our lives. We must not allow a destructive culture to invade and destroy our lives and our work for the heavenly kingdom. The culture of the world enters through our eyes and ears. Review what you are watching on television, viewing on the Internet, listening to, and reading, and evaluate these things according to a healthy kingdom life.

Praying about It

• As you guard your personal culture and become conformed to the nature of the King, make this your daily meditation and prayer: "May the words of my mouth and the meditation of my heart be pleasing in your sight, O LORD, my Rock and my Redeemer" (Psalm 19:14).

"LET YOUR LIGHT SHINE BEFORE MEN, THAT THEY MAY SEE YOUR GOOD DEEDS AND PRAISE YOUR FATHER IN HEAVEN."
—MATTHEW 5:16

Part 4

THE ROLE AND IMPACT OF THE GOVERNOR

Chapter Twelve

MANIFESTING KINGDOM CULTURE

CHAPTER THEME

We have seen that, as citizens of the heavenly kingdom, we should begin to take on the distinguishing characteristics of our new country. While we are still surrounded by the kingdom of darkness, we are to live from the *inside out* rather than from the outside in. We depend on the Governor to instruct and empower us in all the ways of the kingdom—its mind-set, lifestyle, and customs—so that what is within us can be manifested in our attitudes, words, and actions.

There is a distinguishing characteristic of kingdom culture that will enable us to rely more fully on the Governor's leading and guiding. Through it, the Governor not only facilitates our communication with the heavenly kingdom, but he also brings crucial messages from the King to us.

Question for Reflection

1. Do you ever have difficulty communicating your needs or requests to God? In what ways?

Exploring Principles and Purposes

2. What are the four characteristics of all nations? (p. 230)

   (1)

   (2)

   (3)

   (4)

3. Of these four, _____ is the primary manifestation of a nation's culture. (p. 230)

4. There are six reasons this characteristic is so important to a nation. What is the first reason? (p. 231)

5. Culture is _____ in language, because it shapes it. (p. 231)

6. What is the second reason language is important to a nation? (p. 231)

7. Without a common language, the _____ of the people begins to _____. (p. 231)

8. What is the third reason language is important to a nation? (p. 232)

9. What kinds of things is a common language able to transmit that are vital to the health and preservation of a nation? (p. 232)

10. What is the fourth reason language is important? (p. 232)

11. A lack of ability to articulate what they desire to say makes it difficult for people to do what? (p. 232)

12. What is the fifth reason language is important? (p. 232)

13. The sixth reason language is important is that it is the key to _____ _____. In other words, language preserves _____ _____ throughout generations. (p. 233)

14. The power and value of language have important implications for the return of kingdom culture on earth. To begin to understand these implications, we must answer the question, What happened in terms of language and communication when humanity rebelled against the King? (p. 233)

15. The human race retained a common language after the rebellion, which enabled people to communicate easily with one another. What were the circumstances that made it necessary for the King to change humanity's one language to many languages, and to hinder their communication with one another? (pp. 233–235)

16. Confounding humanity's language was the King-Father's way of _____ us until he would one day _____ our unity and communication with him and one another through the _____ of the Governor. (pp. 235–236)

17. What is one of the first things the Governor gives us after we receive his infilling? (p. 236)

18. List two types of heaven-given language. (p. 236)

    (1)

    (2)

19. What does the Governor enable human beings to do through heaven-given languages? (pp. 236–237)

20. What statement did Jesus make that shows us heaven-given languages, or tongues, are part of the evidence of lives that have been reconnected to the heavenly kingdom? (p. 237)

21. The promise of the Father therefore included _____ as well as _____. (p. 237)

22. The Holy Spirit was poured out at Pentecost in fulfillment of the King's promise. The international crowds who were gathered heard the disciples of Jesus speaking the King's plan of restoration in their own languages. List several facts this event revealed. (p. 238)

23. Contrast the incident of the Tower of Babel with the outpouring of the Holy Spirit at Pentecost. (p. 239)

24. We can identify four vital purposes for speaking in heaven-given languages. The first is that tongues provide us with kingdom _____. (p. 240)

25. What is the second purpose of speaking in tongues? (p. 240)

26. What do tongues provide for us when we find it difficult to express our desires and needs to the heavenly government in our earthly language? (p. 240)

27. What is the third purpose of speaking in tongues? (p. 241)

28. The fourth purpose of speaking in tongues is that it is an _____ of our _____ in the kingdom. (p. 241)

29. Many people are uncomfortable with the idea of speaking in tongues and even wonder if tongues are real. This is usually because tongues have been presented to them as something strange or abnormal. What should we realize that will take away this idea of the strangeness of tongues? (p. 242)

30. Why are tongues relevant for us today, as much as they were relevant during the time of the disciples? (p. 242)

31. Dr. Munroe said Lucifer fights especially against the baptism in the Holy Spirit and the outpouring of heavenly gifts. What reason did he give for this? (p. 243)

32. Although you can be a kingdom citizen without speaking in tongues, what disadvantages will you have? (p. 244)

33. Tongues are a _____ line to heaven. (p. 246)

34. List two ways tongues are used in communication. (pp. 246–247)

    (1)

    (2)

35. What are the differences in how these two types of tongues are used for the benefit of kingdom citizens? (pp. 247–248)

36. Speaking in tongues can be a critical key in _____ and _____ other gifts of the Spirit. (p. 249)

37. Dr. Munroe presents ten reasons why every kingdom citizen should speak in tongues. What is the first reason? (p. 249)

38. The second reason for speaking in tongues is that it _____ _____, or _____, our spirits. (p. 250)

39. What is the third reason for speaking in tongues? (p. 250)

40. The fourth reason for speaking in tongues is... [choose one] (p. 251)

    (a) to make sure our own needs are met before others'

    (b) to gain an advantage in dealing with God

    (c) to keep our prayers in line with the King's will

    (d) to coax God into doing something for us

41. The fifth reason for speaking in tongues is to _____ _____. (p. 251)

42. What is the sixth reason? (p. 251)

43. The seventh reason for speaking in tongues is that it enables us to pray for the _____. (p. 252)

44. The eighth reason for speaking in tongues is to give _____ _____. (p. 252)

45. What is the ninth reason? (p. 252)

46. What is the tenth reason for speaking in tongues? (p. 252)

47. This tenth purpose places our _____ under the _____ of the _____ of God. (p. 252)

48. How are tongues a governmental issue in terms of the kingdom of God rather than a religious issue? (p. 254)

Conclusion

Tongues are meant for renewing and building up the lives of kingdom citizens and enabling them to communicate with the heavenly kingdom while receiving power for kingdom purposes. The ability to speak in heaven-given languages is meant for the whole world because it is a gift the King-Son came to provide for all the inhabitants of the earth as part of their reconnection with the kingdom. At Pentecost, Peter said, "The promise is for you and your children and for all who are far off—for all whom the Lord our God will call" (Acts 2:39). Rather than be intimidated by this gift because of erroneous information we have received about it, we should embrace it as a valuable God-given help in living out the kingdom life. It is also our job as kingdom representatives to help people from all backgrounds enter the kingdom of heaven so they may receive this gift and other gifts from the Governor, which will enable them, also, to live the kingdom life on earth.

Applying the Principles of Kingdom Living

Thinking It Over

- What was your perspective of tongues, or heaven-given languages, before reading this book?

- How has your perspective of tongues changed since reading this chapter and answering the questions in this study?

Acting on It

- When we find it difficult to express our needs and desires to God, the Governor will speak for us and through us to the Father, through spiritual communication, including tongues. With tongues, we're not speaking with our minds but through our spirits, and the Spirit communicates every need. If you have not yet received the gift of speaking in heaven-given languages, ask your heavenly Father to give you this gift through the Governor. Then trust him to give it to you and step out in faith to receive it.

- If you have already received the gift of tongues, how often have you been exercising it? Have you been making use of this gift to meet various spiritual needs, such as edification, faith, giving thanks, and spiritual refreshing, that are identified in this chapter? Make a point to include more prayer in tongues in your daily prayers. When you are filled with the Holy Spirit, you can speak in tongues at any time of the day, in order to communicate with your heavenly Father.

Praying about It

- Dr. Munroe said that tongues are our key to overcoming obstacles in many areas of our lives. He gave the example of how praying to the Father in tongues helped him in his studies so that he went from failing grades to becoming a top student. Think about areas in your life that you are struggling with. Bring these areas before the Father in prayer as you pray in heaven-given languages.

- Do you ever wonder if your prayers are according to the will of God? We learned in this chapter that since the Governor knows the mind and will of God, when we pray in heaven-given languages, we can know that the King hears us and that we have the things we have asked for in prayer. The Governor helps us to pray according to the will of the heavenly government. As you pray in tongues, pray in confidence that the Father hears your prayers and is answering them.

TONGUES ARE A DIRECT LINE TO THE HEAVENLY KING.

Chapter Thirteen

THE GOVERNOR'S ADMINISTRATION

CHAPTER THEME

The role of the Governor is to enable kingdom citizens to fulfill their assignment of having dominion over the earth. A significant way in which he does this is by bestowing various types of kingdom authority and power on the citizens as a form of governmental administration on earth. This authority and power can be temporary, for the purpose of fulfilling a specific assignment, or more permanent, to fulfill a certain role in the colony. Through these bestowals, the Governor not only authorizes the presence of the government on earth, but he also reveals the benevolent nature of the King and his desire to give the very best to his citizens.

Question for Reflection

1. Have you ever been given a job or assignment to do, but not the adequate resources with which to do it? How did the job or assignment work out? Compare that experience with one in which you had all the resources you needed. What were the differences in the way you worked, felt, and were effective?

Exploring Principles and Purposes

2. In what way is the Governor responsible for governmental administration over the colony of earth? (p. 255)

3. In light of this responsibility, what are the gifts of the Spirit? (p. 255)

4. What is the nature of the work the King-Son did on earth that he continues in our lives today through the Governor? (p. 255)

5. Authorized power for dominion in the colony is given to kingdom citizens as the Governor _____. (p. 256) Identify a statement in the Constitution of the kingdom, the Scriptures, that explains this. (p. 256)

6. True or False: [circle one] (p. 256)

    Authorized power for dominion in the colony is given for people's private benefit.

7. As the Governor delegates kingdom authority for us, what does he teach us, and how does he do so? (p. 257)

8. Explain the nature of the administration of the gifts. Then identify two statements in the Constitution of the kingdom that confirm this. (p. 257)

9. Authorized power for dominion in the colony is not personal _____. (p. 258)

10. What can happen when kingdom citizens start to believe that the power they have been authorized to use by the Governor actually comes from their own abilities? (p. 258)

11. The Governor delegates power to kingdom citizens in order to address all the _____ of the colony for the _____ _____ of the heavenly kingdom on earth. (p. 258)

12. The kingdom shows its presence on earth by its influence on the _____ and _____ of the world. (p. 259)

13. Some spiritual gifts are given to kingdom citizens in terms of specific roles, such as apostles, prophets, evangelists, pastors, and teachers. What is the purpose of these gifts? (pp. 258–259)

14. How is the authorized power of the Governor involved in the heavenly kingdom's confrontation with the kingdom of darkness? (p. 259)

15. In addition to the gifts that are in the form of specific roles, there are nine gifts of the Holy Spirit, which are listed in Paul's first letter to kingdom citizens living in the city of Corinth. These are *specific administrations* of the Governor on earth. What are these nine gifts, and what three categories do they come under? (p. 259)

    (1)

    (2)

    (3)

16. While there are a _____ of gifts, they have a _____ of purpose. (p. 260)

17. What kinds of things do the revelation gifts address? (p. 260)

18. What is the authorized word of wisdom? (p. 260)

19. How is the word of supernatural wisdom different from wisdom we gain through a knowledge of the Scriptures? (pp. 260–261)

20. In what forms might we receive a word of supernatural wisdom, based on scriptural examples? (p. 261)

21. Who does a word of supernatural wisdom apply to? (p. 262)

22. Through a word of supernatural wisdom, the heavenly government is teaching its citizens regarding how to best _____ governmental _____ and _____ in the colony of earth. (p. 262)

23. How is the authorized word of knowledge different from the authorized word of wisdom? (p. 262)

24. How may a word of knowledge be manifested? (p. 262)

25. True or False: [circle one] (p. 262)

As with a word of wisdom, a word of supernatural knowledge cannot be gained from experience or information, or even a profound acquaintance with the Scriptures.

26. What example from the Scriptures did Dr. Munroe give that demonstrates how the supernatural word of wisdom and the supernatural word of knowledge may overlap? (p. 263)

27. What is the authorized power of faith? (p. 264)

28. In contrast to the supernatural gift of faith, what kinds of faith come through exposure to and application of the Scriptures? (p. 264)

29. There is a close relationship between the gift of faith and what other supernatural gift? (p. 264)

30. What is the authorized power of healing? (p. 265)

31. Healing is the King's commitment to the _____ of his citizens, as well as his program for _____ that _____. (p. 265)

32. The term *gifts of healing* is sometimes translated from the original Greek of the New Testament as "gifts of healings," so that both main words are in the plural. What does this plural usage refer to? What statement about Jesus corresponds to a plural perspective on this gift? (p. 265)

33. Explain how gifts of healing are for the restoration of the whole person. (p. 266)

34. How are supernatural healing, a physician's care, and the body's natural ability to heal distinct channels of healing? (p. 266)

35. What is the distinction between supernatural gifts of healing and healing that comes through exercising faith in the promises of God from Scripture? (p. 266)

36. Dr. Munroe said, "It has been said that healing and compassion go hand in hand. Sympathy alone is ineffective." How is compassion different from sympathy? (p. 267)

37. Summarize the purpose of healing in terms of the administration of the kingdom of heaven on earth. (p. 267)

38. What is the authorized power of miracles, and how is this gift both similar to and distinct from the other gifts? (p. 268)

39. Summarize the purpose of miracles in terms of the administration of the kingdom of heaven on earth. (pp. 268–269)

40. What is the authorized power of prophecy? (p. 269)

41. The three purposes of prophecy are _____, _____, and _____ or _____. (p. 269)

42. Paul indicated that prophecy is the most important gift of all because it edifies kingdom citizens. This concept signifies _____ or _____ people up in the _____ of the kingdom. (pp. 269–270)

43. According to Paul, the gift of prophecy should be… [choose one] (pp. 269–270)

    (a) earnestly forgotten

    (b) earnestly sought

    (c) completely ignored

    (d) considered secondary to tongues

44. Dr. Munroe provided seven guidelines for using the gift of prophecy because, although this gift is vital to kingdom citizens, it has been too often _____. (p. 271)

45. What is the distinction between the gift of prophecy, which all kingdom citizens are encouraged to seek, and the office or specific role of prophet, which is given by the Governor to certain citizens? (p. 271)

46. Summarize the purpose of prophecy in terms of the administration of the kingdom of heaven on earth. (p. 272)

47. What is the authorized power of discernment? (p. 273)

48. Supernatural discernment is… [choose one] (p. 273)

    (a) mind reading or psychic insight

    (b) discerning other people's character or faults

    (c) discerning evil spirits

    (d) discerning both good and evil nonhuman spiritual beings

49. The gift of discernment enables us to tell whether _____ or _____ we receive are from the King or from his enemy. (p. 273)

50. One example of the authorized power of discernment is the ability to discern the _____ _____ of God. (p. 273)

51. Another example of the authorized power of discernment is the revelation of the _____ of a supernatural manifestation (whether it is good or evil). (p. 274)

52. With what two gifts does the authorized power of discernment often work in conjunction? (p. 274)

53. Summarize the purpose of discernment in terms of the administration of the kingdom of heaven on earth. (p. 274)

54. What is the authorized power of special or different kinds of tongues? (p. 275)

55. While devotional tongues is usually _____, and has to do with _____, the gift of different kinds of tongues is _____, and is in regard to _____. (p. 275)

56. Where is the gift of different kinds of tongues manifested, and to whom is it given? (p. 275)

57. What are some guidelines for the proper exercise of the authorized gift of tongues in an assembly of kingdom citizens? (pp. 276–277)

58. Why are tongues not to be spoken out loud in a gathering of kingdom citizens unless there is someone to interpret? (p. 276)

59. How might you know if the gift of tongues is working in you? (p. 276)

60. When a word is truly from the King it will... [choose one] (p. 277)

    (a) condemn people

    (b) discourage people

    (c) build people up

    (d) belittle people

61. True or False: [circle one] (p. 277)

    Like prophecy, special tongues is usually a confirmation, rather than a new direction, regarding something.

62. Why does the gift of tongues sometimes take the form of earthly languages? (p. 277)

63. Summarize the purpose of special tongues in terms of the administration of the kingdom of heaven on earth. (p. 277)

64. What is the authorized power of interpretation of tongues? (pp. 277–278)

65. True or False: [choose one] (p. 278)

    Interpretation of tongues will always be exactly the same length as the message in tongues itself.

66. Summarize the purpose of interpretation of tongues. (p. 278)

67. All authorized power from the Governor comes through the _____ in the Holy Spirit. (p. 279)

Conclusion

Authorized power has to do with effective service on behalf of the heavenly kingdom in the colony of earth. The gifts of the Spirit are therefore not strange, impractical manifestations but very useful endowments. They are given because the King loves us and desires to communicate with us and empower us as we exercise dominion on earth in his name. He does not give us any assignment without providing the means to do it well.

We must remember that we cannot make any gift operate according to our own wills. Each of us should function only in the gifts the Governor gives him. Anyone who exercises a spiritual gift has to subject himself to self-control and the evaluation of the assembly of kingdom citizens. This is for the purpose of keeping order and peace among all citizens. We must be sensitive to the ways in which the Governor is working and not try to force something he isn't doing or quench something he is doing. We should also maintain an open mind to receive whatever gift the Spirit wants to give us, at any time and in any place.

Applying the Principles of Kingdom Living

Thinking It Over

- How have you seen the gifts of the Spirit manifested in your life?

- How have you seen the gifts of the Spirit manifested in an assembly of believers or on other occasions? What were the benefits to those present? Were there any problems or misuses of gifts? If so, how were these addressed?

- Have you ever used the gifts of the Spirit for selfish reasons? What is the true reason for exercising the gifts?

- What new insights about the authorized power of the Governor to kingdom citizens have you gained from this chapter? How might your exercise and experience of the gifts be different now?

Acting on It

- If you have not yet received the baptism in the Holy Spirit, or feel you do not really understand it, review the section on receiving the baptism on pages 279–282. Then, be open to receiving the baptism so you may have the power to serve the King in his kingdom. Remember, if you have not entered the kingdom of God, you must take that first step before receiving the baptism. (See pages 162–164.)

- Paul said prophecy is the most important gift because it edifies kingdom citizens. Review the guidelines for prophecy found on pages 270–271 so you can be prepared to use and help facilitate this gift in an assembly of kingdom citizens.

Praying about It

- Ask your King-Father, in the name of the King-Son, to give you all the authorized gifts of the Governor that are important for fulfilling your role in the kingdom—serving other kingdom believers and reaching out to those who are not yet in the kingdom. As you do, determine to use them faithfully in service for others and not for selfish purposes.

"TO EACH ONE THE MANIFESTATION OF THE SPIRIT IS GIVEN
FOR THE COMMON GOOD."
—1 CORINTHIANS 12:7

NOTES

Chapter Fourteen

WHY THE WHOLE WORLD NEEDS THE GOVERNOR

CHAPTER THEME

The inhabitants of the world today are confronted by global terrorism; economic uncertainty and insecurity; escalating oil prices and fuel costs; the reemerging threat of nuclear weapons; ethnic, cultural, religious, and racial conflicts; political and diplomatic compromise; moral and social disintegration; and a global upsurge in human fear. A spirit of despair is growing and becoming the norm. This fear is compounded by the attempts of humankind, with its limited appreciation for human beings' inherent defects, to address these global conditions through intellectual, religious, scientific, philosophical, and political systems.

Any effective and appropriate help for our world and its plight cannot come from the world itself. We have seen that the restoration of the Creator-King's original intent for the earth can come only through the life and power of the heavenly kingdom, given to us through the Governor. The whole world—each individual in it, as well as the world collectively—needs to acknowledge and experience the return of the Governor.

Questions for Reflection

1. How effective do you think today's leaders are in addressing the problems and needs in the world? Why?

2. How effective are you in addressing your personal problems and needs, and why?

Exploring Principles and Purposes

3. Humanity cannot solve its _____-_____ problems. (p. 284)

4. What kind of help does our world need? (p. 284)

5. The kingdom of heaven is infinitely higher and more powerful than any government on earth, and yet it is _____ _____ _____ _____ _____ _____ _____ _____. (p. 284)

6. If we continue to be victims of our own corrupt nature, what will be the cause? (p. 285)

7. What does the Creator-King's design for humanity's life on earth require? (p. 285)

8. True or False: [circle one] (p. 285)

   The person and role of the Holy Spirit is a religious issue.

   Explain your answer:

9. Each of us needs the Governor for true _____, _____, and _____. (p. 285)

10. It is not the King's intention that his kingdom citizens live in isolation. What is his plan? (p. 286)

11. The world community needs to be led by the _____ if it is to become what it was created to be. (p. 286)

12. What has been the world's corporate response to the presence and influence of the governor, and what has been the result of this? (p. 286)

13. When will we have powerful potential to influence the earth with the nature of the kingdom? (p. 287)

14. What does the heavenly government provide for, encourage, and enable? (p. 287)

15. What is the King's attitude toward his citizens? (p. 288)

16. What does the King's enemy, Lucifer, desire for this world? (p. 288)

17. What did the King-Son do to counteract the power and purposes of Lucifer? (p. 288)

18. What is the message of Jesus and the Scriptures? (p. 290)

19. What is humanity's collective purpose and calling? (p. 290)

20. What will happen as we yield to the Governor's presence and work in our lives? (p. 290)

21. The Spirit gives _____ to the world, in the _____ extent of the word. (p. 291)

22. How is the world ultimately moving toward complete transformation into the King's image and nature? (pp. 291–292)

23. The Holy Spirit is the _____ to the world. (p. 293)

24. Why is the Holy Spirit the most important person on earth? (p. 293)

Conclusion

For healing and restoration, the world urgently needs the light of the kingdom of heaven, which comes only from the King-Son through the Governor. Human beings must return to the life and wholeness of the kingdom. We were created to express the nature of God, and we can relate to and reflect his nature only if we actually have his nature within us through his indwelling Spirit. The meaning of our individual lives, within the larger framework of the community of nations—living out our purposes and exercising our full potential—is therefore totally dependent on our receiving the Governor.

The Constitution of the kingdom says, "But you are a chosen people, a royal priesthood, a holy nation, a people belonging to God, that you may declare the praises of him who called you out of darkness into his wonderful light. Once you were not a people, but now you are the people of God; once you had not received mercy, but now you have received mercy" (1 Peter 2:9–10). May you be reconciled to your Creator-King, receive the Governor into your life, and live as the royal kingdom citizen you were always meant to be!

Applying the Principles of Kingdom Living

Thinking It Over

• What have you learned in this book about the ability of the Holy Spirit, the Governor, to address the fundamental needs and issues of the world?

- What does it mean for you to be part of a community of "kings and priests" who are to reign on earth under the guidance of the Governor? What are the benefits and responsibilities?

Acting on It

- Your ability to live out your unique life purpose and exercise your full potential is totally dependent on receiving the Holy Spirit and allowing him to guide and direct you. Make a commitment now to enter the kingdom of heaven and to live according to the purposes of the King under the direction of the Governor.

- If you are used to thinking of your relationship with the Creator-King as an isolated one, write down some specific ideas of how you can live your life in the heavenly kingdom in conjunction with your fellow-citizens in the realm. As you do, include aspects of kingdom life highlighted in the chapters of this book.

Praying about It

- Daily acknowledge your desire to spread the heavenly kingdom on earth by praying, "Father, 'Not my will, but yours be done'" (Luke 22:42).

- Pray that the King-Father would direct you to those who need to hear the life-giving message of the return of his kingdom. Then trust the Governor to give you the words and actions that will draw others to the Father and into the kingdom.

"BUT SEEK FIRST HIS KINGDOM AND HIS RIGHTEOUSNESS, AND ALL THESE THINGS WILL BE GIVEN TO YOU AS WELL."
—MATTHEW 6:33

NOTES

ANSWER KEY

Chapter One
THE POWER OF INFLUENCE

1. Answers will vary.

2. Answers will vary.

3. Answers will vary.

4. The success of your life depends upon how well you understand and live out the *kingdom life*.

5. The strong influence of Western society's political and social ideas of independence and freedom have permeated the world and affect many areas of people's thinking. The general trend worldwide is toward representational government and self-government. This is a reaction against tyrannical kingdoms and dictators of the past, and democracy is essentially humanity's alternative to perverted kingdoms.

6. The anti-kingdom perspective affects not just styles of government, but also how we view and conduct ourselves in personal relationships, business, media, education, and religion.

7. The kingdom life answers essential questions about our human existence, purpose, and fulfillment.

8. kingdom; colony

9. While many political kingdoms of the past and present seek to force others under their control based on territorial power, greed, or religious doctrine, the transcendent kingdom enables humanity and the personal and corporate progress of the world to develop and thrive.

10. Power is the principal issue of humanity the kingdom life addresses. Power is defined as "the ability to influence and control circumstances": to direct and influence one's life in a positive and fulfilling way.

11. Dr. Munroe defines kingdom as "the governing authority and influence of a sovereign ruler who impacts his territory through his will, purpose, and intentions, which are manifested in the culture, lifestyle, and quality of his citizenry."

12. power; monarch

13. The job of a king's advisors is to take the will of the king, translate it into the law of the land, and make sure it is enacted throughout the kingdom.

14. The goal of a traditional kingdom is to rule and to gain territory. The power of a king is related to the territory he owns.

15. domain; colonies

16. The sovereign's number one goal after gaining a colony is to exercise his personal influence over it.

17. The word *colony* comes from the Latin word *colonia*, derived from *colere*, meaning "to cultivate."

18. The purpose of a colony is to (1) be an extension of the home country in another territory; (2) establish a prototype of the original country in another territory; (3) represent the values, morals, and manners of the home country; (4) manifest the culture and lifestyle of the original nation.

19. (b) the presence of the absent king in the colony

20. The governor was the most important person in the colony because he was the direct instrument of the transformation of the colony into the kingdom.

21. Clarifies the king's desires, ideas, intent, purposes, will, and plans: (4) *interpretation*

    Conveys what the king wants the colony to know or receive: (2) *communication*

    Shares rule with the king: (6) *partnership*

    Provides the kingdom access to the colony: (1) *relationship*

    Acts on behalf of the king to the colony, and on behalf of the colony to the king: (3) *representation*

    Exercises authority to execute the king's desires and commands for the colony. (5) *power*

22. True

23. False (The royal governor always came from the home kingdom.)

24. False (While the governor represented both king and colonists, he was accountable only to the king.)

25. True

26. True

27. False (The colonists were to take on both the culture and history of the kingdom.)

28. False (Kingdom citizenry was a privilege granted by the king himself. Otherwise, colonists were subjects. The governor prepared subjects for citizenship and recommended them when he felt they were ready for the rights and privileges of being full citizens.)

29. False (The royal governor lived in the colony full-time; the kingdom built a residence there for him to live in.)

30. True

31. The governor was valuable (1) as the presence of the kingdom government; (2) for representing the government; (3) for the enablement of the colony; (4) for protection; (5) for his ability to know and communicate the mind of the king; (6) for enabling the colony's citizens and subjects to fulfill the will of the kingdom.

32. Jesus of Nazareth said, "The time has come….The kingdom of God is near" (Mark 1:15).

33. imminent; influence

34. The transcendent kingdom has properties that are similar to, but go beyond, those of traditional earthly kingdoms.

Chapter Two
THE ADAMIC ADMINISTRATION

1. Answers will vary.

2. Answers will vary.

3. The first government on earth came from a kingdom outside it.

4. (1) The territory of earth was created by the home country rather than taken by force. It was not anyone else's possession beforehand; (2) there were no inhabitants on earth at first, which was designed with them in mind; it was specifically prepared for those who would live here; (3) the original inhabitants were not of a different culture from the home country but were actually the offspring of the King himself.

5. (1) The home country desired to expand the realm of its influence by bringing the nature, mind-set, and purposes of the kingdom to the colony of earth; (2) the King's Governor was present in the colony to oversee the transformation process. He was to guide the King's children—his local governors—who were to convert the colony into a replica of the kingdom.

6. The eternal King of an unseen kingdom conceptualized and made the entire physical universe. The first book of Moses says, "In the beginning God [the Creator-King] created the heavens and the earth [the physical universe]" (Genesis 1:1).

7. By creation rights, the universe belongs to the Creator-King.

8. An orderly government of vast ability and power maintains the universe.

9. invisible; physical

10. The invisible kingdom is the governing influence of God over the territory of earth, impacting and influencing it with his will, his purpose, and his intent.

11. kingdom; home country; colony

12. Human beings were created to have the very nature of the Creator-King and his kingdom.

13. The Creator-King extended rulership of earth to humanity, his royal "children."

14. The words *image* and *likeness* describe and define our design, capacity, potential, and value as human beings made to reflect the personhood of our Creator.

15. The only way a kingdom can function perfectly is if it is ruled by a perfect king who will not betray his citizens through corruption or oppression.

16. benevolence

17. (c) its citizens

18. (1) The Creator gave human beings—who possessed his spiritual nature and characteristics—physical bodies so they could function in the physical world he had prepared specifically for them; (2) the Creator breathed into human beings his very Spirit, animating and empowering them to fulfill their calling on earth.

19. The breath of the Spirit ignited life in Adam (1) in the invisible spirit of man, which, being made in the image of God, is eternal; (2) in the soul of man—meaning the total human consciousness of his mind, will, and emotions; and (3) in his physical body, which became a living vessel housing the spirit and soul.

20. Man's soul and body gave him an awareness of his earthly environment.

21. Man's spirit—through the Spirit of God dwelling within him—gave him an awareness of his Creator-King and the ability to communicate directly with the heavenly government.

22. Governor; proceeded; dwelled

23. The Governor enabled humanity to receive, know, and carry out the Creator-King's will.

24. (a) man's spirit

25. The true, kingdom-built residence in which the Governor lives, and from which he governs the colony of earth, is the physical bodies of human beings within whom he dwells.

26. False. (As members of the King's royal family, human beings were not subjects but had the full status of citizens of the kingdom.)

27. The assignment of the Adamic Administration was to have dominion over the earth and colonize it for the kingdom under the heavenly Governor.

28. To have dominion means to govern, to rule, to control, to manage, to lead, to affect, and to impact.

29. Humanity's job was to execute heaven's policies, legislation, and oversight on earth—to cultivate the life of the heavenly kingdom, manage the earth's natural resources, rule over the animals, govern wisely and justly, and keep everything in order.

30. The key to humanity's effective rulership on earth was a benevolent governing that had the best interests of the kingdom and its citizens at heart.

31. The Governor fulfilled the requirements of delegated authority for humanity in the following ways: (1) the Governor came from the King and was the only one who could suitably transform the colony into the home country. He knew the King's heart, mind, desires, will, and intent; (2) the Governor was committed to carrying out the King's purposes in the territory.

32. Human beings were suited to transform the colony of earth into the nature of the heavenly kingdom because (1) they were made in the image and likeness of the Creator-King; (2) they had the Creator-King's own personal presence—His Spirit—living within them. In this way, the earth would be intimately related to the home country in nature and purpose.

33. bridge; channel; communication

34. The presence of the Holy Spirit within human beings gave them the (1) authority and (2) ability to have dominion over their environment. These two things address the primary issue of power for humanity.

35. Human beings desire power because they were designed to fulfill their original assignment as vice governors on earth.

36. (a) practical; (c) the rule of an eternal King over his territory; (e) the relationship between a King and his ruler-children; (f) the transformation of colony into kingdom

Chapter Three
DECLARATION OF INDEPENDENCE

1. Answers will vary.

2. Answers will vary.

3. The heavenly kingdom's plan to expand its realm on earth was disrupted when a rebellion that started in the home country spread to the colony.

4. The rebellion was instigated by one of the King's top generals, Lucifer, who had attempted a coup of the heavenly kingdom and been banished, along with his followers. His motivation was to insult the King, thwart the purposes of the kingdom, and usurp the colony.

5. Lucifer's plan was to sever the relationship between the King's children and their Father and separate the citizens of the colony from their true government. He infiltrated the colony's government using craftiness and deceit.

6. The strategy for accomplishing the plan was to promote a spirit of rebellion and independence. Subtly questioning the integrity and goodwill of the Sovereign, Lucifer seduced the King's children to disregard his authority over the colony and encouraged them in an act of insurrection.

7. (a) for the children's protection

8. The children's response was (1) contrary to the nature and desires of the King; (2) a corruption of their own nature, which had been made in the King's likeness.

9. serious breech of faith; departure

10. The children of the King violated the legal contract the government of heaven had established with human beings; their rebellion amounted to treason.

11. Sin is rebellion against the essential nature and authority of the heavenly government.

12. Lucifer would transform the colony into a kingdom of darkness.

13. The worst result of the children's rejection of the King and his nature was losing their essential source of life as human beings—the King's Spirit.

14. Since the Spirit of the King gave life to man's spirit, soul, and body, his absence led to human beings' spirits and souls being cut off from the home country, and their physical bodies began to die a slow death. Spiritually and soulically, they were already dead to the King and his kingdom.

15. recalled

16. The loss of the Governor meant the loss of the environment of the kingdom on earth. Earth's environment changed to the antithesis of the heavenly kingdom.

17. inside out; outside in

18. Human beings became dependant on their five physical senses.

19. (c) a limited perspective on life's realities

20. Human beings were never intended to interpret the physical world from itself but from the spiritual reality of the kingdom. The things that are seen were made from things that

are not seen, and the only way to truly understand something is to relate to how it was made and who made it.

21. The Governor is not only vital for our relationship with the invisible King, but also for understanding our own humanity. Only through the Governor can we know why we are really here and how to interpret the world in which we live. We can't express the King's nature unless we are in relationship with him, and the Governor provided that relationship. To be true and complete human beings, we must somehow become reconnected to and re-indwelled by the Holy Spirit.

22. power; authority

23. From the King's standpoint, the self-government of human beings meant the spiritual death of his beloved children who were meant to carry on the family name and legacy.

24. The harsh realities of self-government were the introduction of fear, a survival mind-set, and the knowledge of the inevitability of death.

25. The loss of the Governor left human beings in a state of rebellion that does not have the purposes of the kingdom at heart.

26. Human beings fall short of the essential nature of God and everything that makes him praiseworthy. We have distorted the image of the Creator-King's perfection within us. All our efforts to execute government on earth in personal and corporate ways fall deeply short as well.

27. Humanity created a culture of darkness that can be described as man's inhumanity to man. It includes adultery, incest, abuse, domestic violence, and murder; it destroys young and old, strong and weak. The abuse and destruction afflict families, communities, businesses, and government—the whole realm of human existence.

28. Trying to run the planet without the King's nature has led to a breakdown in human authority and power to address vital issues. It is the source of the world's poverty, genocide, terrorism, political corruption, drug addiction, broken homes, and every kind of evil that can be named. We have created a state of rebellion and confusion.

29. (d) promised the return of the Governor and earth's restoration

30. The bottom line in all people's search for power and meaning in life is that they are actually seeking the return of the Governor to their lives, even though they may not realize it.

31. The King's plan was to send an Offspring, to be born in the colony, who would restore kingdom influence to the colony. This Offspring would crush the power of the realm of darkness, take back the kingdom authority that was stolen by Lucifer, and restore power and authority to humanity. Human beings would be reinstated as local

rulers on behalf of the heavenly kingdom by the reappointment of the Governor to the colony of earth.

32. dysfunctional; complete

Chapter Four
THE PROMISE OF THE GOVERNOR'S RETURN

1. Answers will vary.

2. Answers will vary.

3. restoration of his kingdom on earth

4. The principal purpose is the restoration of the Governor to the colony of earth.

5. The universal theme of the Old Testament is the restoration of the key to *humanity's* existence, the reestablishment of true life for *every human being* on the planet.

6. They could be and do what the King originally intended for them, and fulfill their remarkable purpose and potential.

7. (1) They are a continual reminder of the promise of the Governor's restoration; (2) they depict the King's intervention in the lives of specific families on earth to preserve a lineage for the Offspring who would restore the Governor; (3) they depict a prototype of the restoration of the kingdom of heaven on earth; (4) they expose the fact that only the Governor himself can reconnect the earthly colony to its heavenly government; (5) they foretell the coming of the Offspring who will personally reconcile the children-citizens to the King and authorize the return of the Governor.

8. (1) pure—set apart specifically and purely for a certain use; (2) devoted or dedicated—one's loyalty is not tainted by other loyalties or ulterior motives

9. The Creator-King's holiness means that he is true to himself; he is faithful and consistent in who he is, what he desires, what he says, and what he does. He has complete integrity.

10. It means "to be one with yourself," never contradicting your word or your nature.

11. The Governor not only had to leave humanity, but also was unable to return because human beings were no longer pure in motive or integrated in themselves, and consequently were no longer set apart for the King or in agreement with him. The Governor is a pure Spirit and cannot live in intimate relationship with humanity in that environment.

12. state of being

13. (1) He implemented a program that allowed the Governor to come *upon* people, although not *within* them, so as not to violate his integrity. *His Spirit could come upon any*

person who chose to submit to the influence of the heavenly government; (2) He initiated the sacrificial system, which allowed the Governor to work on earth through a special nation of people who were meant to be a prototype of the return of the kingdom to the whole world; (3) The King himself would come to earth to restore integrity to humanity, and thus provide a way for the Governor to again live *within* human beings on a permanent basis.

14. The Offspring was the King himself who was coming to earth, incarnated as a human being, to restore the Governor.

15. King-Son

16. lineage

17. The Governor's presence on earth through the submission of individuals to the heavenly government was always accompanied by the manifestation of kingdom influence over the earth's environment.

18. From the point of view of the heavenly kingdom, miracles were not extraordinary but rather natural outcomes of the influence of the heavenly government in the lives of those yielded to the King.

19. The culture of the world became so evil it had to be virtually destroyed by the worldwide flood in order to preserve a lineage for the Offspring. Noah and his family were preserved because Noah had a heart that was obedient to the Creator-King.

20. The King's words to Noah after the flood were almost exactly the same that he had spoken to Adam: "Be fruitful and increase in number and fill the earth" (Genesis 9:1). These words revealed the King was continuing the same program with Noah's family he had begun with Adam and Eve. He did not change his original purpose for humanity after their rebellion but was working on a plan to restore it.

21. (1) Isaac would be the beginning of a great nation, which in turn would be a prototype of what the kingdom of heaven on earth was supposed to look like; (2) one of Isaac's descendants would be the promised Offspring.

22. holiness

23. *Righteousness* refers to "right standing" or "right alignment" with evident authority.

24. Jacob; Israel, meaning "Prince with God."

25. Jacob's (Israel's) twelve sons became the twelve tribes of Israel. The lineage was carried on through Jacob's son Judah.

26. The Israelite nation was not preserved in order to create a religion but to be an instrument in the hand of the King's unfolding purposes to reconcile the whole world to himself and to restore the Governor.

27. The Israelites were called and set apart as a special nation so they could rediscover the King and his ways. They were to become a nation with the holy (dedicated) purpose of being a "kingdom of priests and a holy nation" (Exodus 19:6). This would enable them to help fulfill the King's plan of restoration for the world. The nation as a whole was to be a prototype of what the King would do for all who were submitted to his Governor and were ruling their homes, communities, and nations under his guidance.

28. *Kingdom* indicates governing responsibility, while the role of the priest was to help people become realigned with the heavenly government. In essence, priestly work involves lining up with true authority, and kingdom work has to do with executing rulership under that authority.

29. priest; ruler

30. When the Israelite people first came out of Egyptian slavery, they had forgotten much about the King and his ways. They had lost a clear conception of his nature and will. He therefore gave them instructions for living, called the law. This was a comprehensive picture of how they were supposed to think and act as a kingdom of priests and rulers living in integrity, according to the King's nature. Their King wanted them to understand how his Spirit thought and how his kingdom worked so they could stay in alignment with him.

31. If the Israelites obeyed the King's laws, they would attract his Spirit because they would be living in holiness and be in harmony with his nature. The King would provide for them and protect them; they would have everything they needed, and they would never be defeated by their enemies.

32. The nation of Israel didn't live up to its high purpose. The people rejected the laws of the King over and over throughout their history. They went out of alignment with the King and failed to be an example to other nations of the kingdom of heaven on earth.

33. (c) exist in the spirit of people's minds

34. The Israelites had forsaken their calling to be a nation of priests, perpetually aligned with the King. The priesthood, sacrifices, and rituals were therefore for the purpose of restoring and realigning the people with God when they rebelled against him and violated his kingdom standards, so they could be what they were originally called to be. In the system of sacrifices, the blood atoned for the violations against the kingdom law the people had committed. They were God's (temporary) provision for realigning the people with him so his Spirit could return and intervene on the earth once more through the nation of Israel.

35. presence; them; rebellious

36. The people's desire for a king indicated a lack of alignment with the King and a complete misunderstanding of their calling as a nation of kingdom rulers. This was an additional rejection of their heavenly king.

37. Ultimately, the King used the line of Israelite kings to preserve the lineage for his Son's coming to earth.

38. Many of Israel's kings became corrupt. The priesthood also became corrupt. So the Creator-King raised up people from within the Israelite nation, at various times, who could speak to both priests and kings on behalf of the heavenly kingdom. The King's Spirit would come upon the prophet, and the prophet would tell the king and the priests to correct themselves so they could correct the nation and bring the people back in alignment with their heavenly King. In this way, the nation could return to being the prototype of the kingdom of heaven. The Israelite nation could then correct the nations of the world, for the ultimate purpose of redeeming the whole earth.

39. The King of the eternal, invisible kingdom was going to come to earth himself and reclaim his lost citizens and property. When the colony was regained, he would set up his government on earth again and recommission his Spirit as Governor once more.

40. Over the centuries, specific prophets, as well as other leaders in Israel, such as Moses and David, spoke messages from the King announcing that he himself would reestablish his kingdom in the colony of earth.

41. (d) all of the above

42. The "day of the Lord" (Joel 2:11) referred to the era or the time when the King would come to earth.

43. "The kingdom of heaven is near" (Matthew 3:2) meant that the King's government was imminent because the King had come to earth.

44. When the King baptized people with the Holy Spirit and fire, he would align them with the kingdom again. The Spirit's coming would no longer be a temporary appearance but a permanent one. The Governor would burn out every false mind-set and philosophy that alienated the citizens from the heavenly kingdom. The earth would be a colony of holiness and power again because its inhabitants would finally have the Spirit of holiness and power living within them once more.

Chapter Five
THE REBIRTH OF A KINGDOM

1. Answers will vary.

2. Answers will vary.

3. promise; rebirth; arrival

4. The Spirit of the King conceived God the Son or the King-Son, whose earthly name was Jesus, in the womb of Mary. Mary was what we might call a surrogate mother for the eternal and invisible God's entrance into the physical world as a human being.

5. The King-Son was filled with the Spirit when he was conceived in the womb of Mary. The Governor was resident in the body of Jesus until the rest of humanity could be prepared to receive him as well, through Jesus' provision.

6. divine

7. human

8. Jesus the man was not infected by the rebellious nature of humanity.

9. Jesus and everything about him was set apart and devoted to the King-Father.

10. John the Baptist said, "God gives the Spirit without limit [to Jesus]" (John 3:34). The Holy Spirit within Jesus was limitless in presence and power.

11. King-Son; Governor; heavenly kingdom

12. (1) Jesus was the one who would take away the sin of the world (making it possible for the citizens to be fully aligned with the heavenly kingdom); (2) Jesus was the Son of God (he came directly from the King-Father and was one with him); (3) the Spirit came down from heaven and *remained* on him (Jesus had the total sanction of the King-Father).

13. one; three

14. King; King; human form

15. The King's mission on earth was to restore holiness to men and women so they could again be a suitable environment for the Holy Spirit to dwell in.

16. The purpose and nature of the kingdom was (1) the reconciliation of the earth's inhabitants to the King-Father, so that it was possible once more for human beings to be his children, and (2) the reign of heaven returning to earth through the Governor's presence and power operating in the lives of the King's children.

17. The inhabitants of the colony of earth had been ransacking the King's territory—stealing, lying, abusing, killing one another, living their lives outside the nature of the kingdom.

18. The King came to reclaim the earth because, as the psalmist David, king of Israel, wrote, "The earth is the Lord's, and everything in it" (Psalm 24:1). He came to recover all of creation as its legal owner.

19. The King-Son called Lucifer a "thief" and a "strong man": "The thief comes only to steal and kill and destroy; I have come that they may have life, and have it to the full" (John 10:10). "How can one enter a strong man's house and plunder his goods, unless he first binds the strong man? And then he will plunder his house" (Matthew 12:29 NKJV). The King-Son came to *bind* the strongman, Lucifer, so he could retake the house and give it back to the children of the household—the King's children.

20. The King-Son came to fulfill what the first Adam had failed to do. He lived a life in total harmony with the King-Father, his kingdom, and the kingdom's purposes on earth.

21. The kingdom of heaven can be called *a family of kings* because, through Jesus, human beings can be restored as vice governors in the world, earthly kings who rule under the direction of the Spirit of the King—the Royal Governor. This is what the nation of Israel was meant to demonstrate as a prototype: "a kingdom of priests and a holy nation" (Exodus 19:6).

22. the kingdom of heaven

23. place; influence

24. Lucifer tried to get Jesus to substitute the kingdoms of the world for the kingdom of heaven, which is basically the same thing with which he had tempted Adam and Eve. This would allow him to maintain his oppressive domination and destruction of the earth.

25. The King-Son was totally loyal to the kingdom, and he countered Lucifer's temptation by rebuking him with the words of the King-Father, which were first given to the Israelites after they came out of Egypt, "'Worship the Lord your God, and serve him only'" (Matthew 4:10).

26. Baptism meant you were publicly declaring you believed in a particular teacher and his philosophy. When a person was baptized, he was signaling that he was changing his thinking and actions and aligning them with the views and life of the teacher he had committed himself to follow.

27. (b) pupil

28. school of thought

29. False. (When you were baptized in the name of your master teacher, you were saying, "I am choosing you above every other available teacher, philosopher, rabbi, and leader, and I am publicly declaring that I am submitting to your school of thought. I'm going to be associated with you *only*.")

30. When the Creator of heaven and earth himself came to earth as a man, he entered the culture of the day and presented himself in such a way that the people would understand the life-changing nature of his message and its requirement of total commitment to him.

31. (c) the same as Jesus' message

32. Jesus was baptized by John to demonstrate to the people of the world that his teaching was not independent of John's; rather, he was in total harmony with it. He needed to publicly declare he belonged to the school of the kingdom of heaven, and that he was fully integrated with the mind and ways of the kingdom. In fact, Jesus himself was the *fulfillment* of the teaching

of John who, as the faithful prophet of the King-Father, was proclaiming the message of the kingdom and preparing the way for the King-Son's appearance in the world.

33. After Jesus was baptized, the Holy Spirit—the Governor—descended on him. "At that moment heaven was opened, and he saw the Spirit of God descending like a dove and lighting on him. And a voice from heaven said, 'This is my Son, whom I love; with him I am well pleased'" (Matthew 3:16–17). The King-Father was confirming, "This one has the Holy Spirit; he is my Son, and he is fully integrated with my thoughts and ways. He is the one who will restore my Spirit to the earth."

34. "This is my Son, whom I love. Listen to him!" (Mark 9:7).

35. We are followers of Jesus when we have decided to identify with the life and message of the King-Son and submit to him as our Master Teacher in the school of the kingdom of heaven.

36. The baptism with the Holy Spirit is the consummation of identification with the King and his kingdom, as well as a reception of the power of the heavenly kingdom. The Holy Spirit is the personification of the heavenly government. To be baptized in this way means you are immersed in kingdom philosophy and lifestyle, and that it has total influence over your thoughts and actions.

37. The Creator-King declared, concerning the rebellious inhabitants of earth, "My thoughts are not your thoughts, neither are your ways my ways....As the heavens are higher than the earth, so are my ways higher than your ways and my thoughts than your thoughts" (Isaiah 55:8–9).

38. message; fullness; power

39. Jesus' entire life on earth was evidence of kingdom rulership. Everything he said or did was the administration of the King-Father's will through the power of the Governor within him.

40. The administration of the kingdom could be seen whenever Jesus healed someone who was sick (power over the effects of humanity's rebellion), delivered someone who was possessed by an agent of Lucifer (power over the kingdom of darkness), fed thousands by multiplying small amounts of food (power over the natural world), or raised people from the dead (power to give life). These acts were demonstrations of kingdom power over circumstances.

41. (a) only what the King-Father initiated

42. The only way the holiness of human beings could be restored was through a sacrifice.

43. The ultimate reason for the King's incarnation was to take the punishment of death for humanity's rebellion against the heavenly kingdom, so the earth's inhabitants could be

reconciled to the King. The Old Testament animal sacrifices were only temporary. They were not equitable blood payment for the rebellion and the culture of hatred and death human beings had brought to earth. Only human blood could make restitution for the rebellion and bloodshed of humanity. Instead of making the people pay for their rebellion with their own blood, however, the Father sent the Son to earth as a human being to pay for it with his blood.

44. Jesus was able to be the ultimate sacrifice because he was holy—he was fully integrated, devoted, and set apart for the King-Father and lived a perfect life.

45. (d) the result of his laying down his life voluntarily

46. The King-Father gave the King-Son authority to lay down his life and authority to take it up again.

47. When the penalty of death for the rebellion of humanity was paid, Jesus was raised from the dead.

48. newness of life. (See Romans 6:4 NKJV.)

49. Because Jesus completed the work of restoration, the glory (nature) of the kingdom of heaven was released and began to spread throughout the earth.

50. rebellion (or independence); yieldedness; obey

51. Each human being must make a personal decision to commit to Jesus' kingdom school and enter into the kingdom by accepting his sacrifice to break the spirit of rebellion and by desiring to realign with the King. As he does this, he will receive the nature of the kingdom within.

52. citizens; earth

53. The Holy Spirit is the source of the power of the kingdom in our lives.

54. personified

55. "Your kingdom come, your will be done on earth as it is in heaven" essentially means, "May the King Father's influence, will, intent, and laws be done on earth—the colony—as they are in heaven—the home country."

56. transform; colony; kingdom

Chapter Six
A KING'S LOVE FOR HIS CITIZENS

1. Answers will vary.

2. Answers will vary.

3. Answers will vary.

4. unqualified love

5. The King-Son loved the people of the world so much that he voluntarily limited himself in significant ways in order to restore them to the kingdom.

6. representation

7. love

8. Jesus limited himself by (1) emptying himself so we could be full; becoming poor so we could be rich; (2) placing himself under the restrictions of a world of space and time so we could be connected to the eternal kingdom; (3) subjecting himself to law so he could free those under it; (4) submitting to physical death so we could have eternal life.

9. The King-Son temporarily emptied himself of his heavenly power, glory, and riches to live as a physical, earthly being dependent on the King-Father for everything through the Spirit.

10. The King-Son—who owns the universe—limited himself to a small region on a small planet during an earthly life of thirty-three years, where he could be in only one place at a time. He lived there, died there, rose again there, and even ascended to heaven from there. Eternity allowed itself to be limited within time, so that those in time could be reconnected to the eternal kingdom.

11. The law of Moses and the sacrificial system had been instituted for those who were disconnected from the King. The King-Son had full access to, and total communion with, the King-Father; yet he submitted himself to all the requirements of the law so that he could perfectly fulfill them. Then, when we receive his perfect sacrifice on our behalf, we are enabled to obey God through the indwelling Holy Spirit. The King-Son also temporarily submitted himself to the limitations of the laws of nature in this physical world, in order to give back dominion power to humanity.

12. The King-Son allowed himself to be limited in a physical human body, and to be limited by the experience of physical death, even though he had no sin. He took all our sins on himself and died in our place because only another human being could be a viable substitute for humanity.

13. The King-Son *chose* to die for the inhabitants of earth in order to bring them into freedom.

14. Jesus was resurrected—never to be limited by death again. He conquered death, taking away its sting from humanity. When we enter into the kingdom through Jesus' sacrifice for us, we receive eternal life, and death can't keep our physical bodies in the grave forever. Death has no ultimate claim on us because Jesus has already paid the punishment of death for us. Paul wrote, "By his power God raised the Lord from the dead, and he will raise us also" (1 Corinthians 6:14).

15. Now that the King-Son has returned to the King-Father and sent the Governor to us, the kingdom and its influence can be all over the world at the same time through the Spirit, who lives in all kingdom citizens. Jesus explained to his disciples he *had* to go back to heaven so he could reappoint the Governor from the heavenly kingdom to be with them always. This would bring about unlimited kingdom influence on earth because they would be *indwelled* with the Holy Spirit. The Spirit wouldn't be with them only in a limited way, such as Jesus had to be as a human being when he ministered to limited numbers of people at a time or was alone praying to the Father. Today, the Holy Spirit can be with us continually, day and night, in all situations.

16. If the King-Son hadn't gone to the cross and been resurrected, we would still be trapped in rebellion and in the kingdom of darkness.

17. If the King-Son hadn't returned to the heavenly home country and sent the Governor to fill us, the kingdom of God would not have been able to fully return to the earth.

18. Jesus said, "Your Father has been *pleased* to give you the kingdom" (Luke 12:32, emphasis added). It delighted the King-Father to restore the Governor to us.

19. priceless

Chapter Seven
RESTORING THE CONNECTION

1. Answers will vary.

2. Answers will vary.

3. the giving of the Governor

4. Shortly after his resurrection, Jesus came to the room where his disciples had gathered, and said, "'As the Father has sent me, I am sending you.' And with that he breathed on them and said, 'Receive the Holy Spirit'" (John 20:21–22).

5. This giving of the Spirit was very similar to what the Creator did when he first made Adam (man) a living human being. The Scripture says, "The Lord God formed the man from the dust of the ground and breathed into his nostrils the breath of life, and the man became a living being" (Genesis 2:7).

6. Jesus said, "Receive the Holy Spirit," rather than just "receive the breath of life." He was indicating that the breath of life *is* the Holy Spirit; the Governor *is* the life of humanity. Without Him, even though our bodies may be physically alive for a limited length of time, we are dead to the kingdom, to the heavenly influence we were created to live in, and to the Creator-King himself.

7. lost

8. In breathing on his disciples, Jesus reconnected humanity to the kingdom of heaven. He was literally bringing his disciples into identity with heaven's government. He was renewing human beings' standing and authority in the kingdom; they were restored to their original assignment as vice governors of earth. The disciples of Jesus were the first human beings after Jesus to receive the Governor resident within them again.

9. False. (Jesus' central message was the kingdom, and after his resurrection, his message continued to be the kingdom. Luke the physician wrote, "After his suffering, he showed himself to these men [his disciples] and gave many convincing proofs that he was alive. He appeared to them over a period of forty days *and spoke about the kingdom of God*" [Acts 1:3, emphasis added]).

10. We can know the kingdom of God is on earth now because wherever the Governor is, the kingdom is present. The Governor is resident within kingdom citizens on earth, and therefore the kingdom is present on earth. Jesus said concerning the Holy Spirit, "The kingdom of God is within you" (Luke 17:21).

11. The disciples had received the Governor into their lives and were reconnected to the kingdom. But they still needed to be connected to the kingdom's *power,* which the King would soon send them from the heavenly country when he poured out the Governor onto them.

12. Being connected to the power of the kingdom is what John meant when he said Jesus would baptize with the Holy Spirit and with fire. (See Matthew 3:11.)

13. Jesus told his disciples, "Stay in the city until you have been clothed with power from on high" (Luke 24:49), and "You will receive power when the Holy Spirit comes on you" (Acts 1:8).

14. We are to receive our power from the heavenly country, from a place *outside* this world, because this world is controlled by the kingdom of darkness. Again, the King-Son sent the Governor to earth *from the throne of the Father,* just as a royal governor was sent to a colony from the throne of the king to carry on the work of the sovereign there.

15. Luke the physician recorded, "When the day of Pentecost came, they were all together in one place. Suddenly a sound like the blowing of a violent wind came from heaven and filled the whole house where they were sitting. They saw what seemed to be *tongues of fire* that separated and came to rest on each of them. All of them were filled with the Holy Spirit and began to speak in other tongues as the Spirit enabled them" (Acts 2:1–4, emphasis added).

16. When the Holy Spirit was poured out on Jesus' followers, they were given power to speak in the variety of languages spoken by the Jewish people who had come to Jerusalem, from a number of countries, to celebrate the feast of Pentecost. The heavenly government

gave them the ability to communicate the message that the kingdom of God had fully come so that people of many nations could hear this momentous news.

17. Their speaking in these languages was an evidence that they were connected to the King and their assignment to bring the kingdom of heaven to earth. Jesus had previously told his disciples, "And these signs will accompany those who believe: In my name they will...speak in new tongues..." (Mark 16:17).

18. fulfilled

19. influence; government

20. What separates the kingdom of heaven from all other philosophies, belief systems, and religions is that its citizens have within them the Holy Spirit. Religions have doctrines, tenets, and lists of *dos* and *don't*s, but they don't have the indwelling Spirit.

21. people; ways; spheres; life

22. The King wants you to represent his kingdom in the midst of the kingdom of darkness that currently controls this world, so others can be reconciled to the heavenly government, also.

23. The word *greater* in this statement has to do with magnitude, not quality. We could never improve on the quality of the works of Jesus. But when we are aligned with the mind and will of the Father, and his purposes are foremost in our lives, Jesus promised, "And I will do whatever you ask in my name, so that the Son may bring glory to the Father" (John 14:13). All who have received the Spirit will collectively multiply Jesus' works in the world, and the nature of the heavenly government will be spread throughout the colony.

24. reality; possible

25. The Governor is the most important person on earth because he is the only one who can connect us to King and, through us, dispel the kingdom of darkness with his kingdom of light.

Chapter Eight
REINSTATING THE GOVERNOR

1. Answers will vary.

2. Answers will vary.

3. The reality of the new birth is that there is a continuous reservoir of God's Spirit within us, much like a spring forever bubbling up with fresh, clean, life-giving water. As we continually drink deeply from this water of the Spirit within us, we will constantly be connected to the life of the kingdom.

4. reconnects; government

5. When we receive the Holy Spirit in our lives, it is like a "deposit" showing we now belong to the King and that he gives us an inheritance in his heavenly kingdom.

6. restores; citizenship

7. reinstates; kingdom

8. (b) the more the kingdom influence should be felt on earth

9. communication; access

10. admittance; influence

11. nature; king

12. The baptism in the Spirit prepares us for earth—for our restored dominion assignment to make the earth into a replica of heaven.

13. Jesus said concerning the baptism in the Holy Spirit, "Whoever believes in me, as the Scripture has said, *streams of living water will flow from within him*" (John 7:38, emphasis added). The baptism is like a forceful river; it is like waterpower that is harnessed as energy to run equipment, such as in a mill, for the betterment of humanity and its needs.

14. dominion

15. Power is the ability to influence and control circumstances.

16. represent; government

17. The gifts of the Spirit are evidence of the presence, authority, and power of the government of God on earth.

18. prove

19. display; glory

20. (d) transcend human language and culture

21. demonstrate; citizenship

22. The baptism is like a passport in that it both identifies us as belonging to the King and gives us credibility in carrying out the work of the kingdom.

23. The only one who can exercise the power of the heavenly kingdom is a recognized authority of the kingdom—one authorized by the King through his indwelling Spirit.

24. Paul's authority in the heavenly kingdom was respected and obeyed by agents of the kingdom of darkness.

25. Dr. Munroe presented these steps: (1) Repent. Change your mind about how you have been living and desire to live by the standards of the heavenly kingdom. (2) Receive the forgiveness provided through Jesus' sacrifice, which releases you from the guilt of your sins.

26. The kingdom life is seeking the good of the kingdom first and allowing the King to provide for all your needs as you serve him in the authority and power he gives you through the heavenly Governor.

Chapter Nine
RESULTS OF RECONNECTION

1. Answers will vary.

2. The first result of reconnection is a restored relationship with the King-Father.

3. source; rights; privileges

4. We must acknowledge to our heavenly Father, (1) "I came from you"; (2) "I must be sustained by you; I depend on you." We place the obligation for our sustenance upon God.

5. The second result of reconnection is entrance into a nondiscriminatory and nonpartisan kingdom.

6. The coming of the Governor affirmed the value and access to the kingdom of all people who will receive him, including men and women; the young, middle-aged, and elderly; people of any social status; people of every nation, race, ethnicity; people of religious or non-religious backgrounds. All are welcome to enter into and serve the kingdom.

7. everyone; filled

8. (c) a steward of kingdom authority and power

9. The third result of reconnection is that it gives us a restored ability to influence the world around us.

10. (1) Legal or delegated-authority gives you the *right* to do something; (2) Ability-authority gives you the power or wherewithal to back up the authority by accomplishing the mandate.

11. False. (You will not have the resources or the power to see much accomplished.)

12. resources; heaven

13. As kingdom citizens, we are to act in the *name* of Jesus, the King-Son to whom all authority has been given by the Father, when we work on behalf of the kingdom through the power of the Governor.

14. Jesus said, "I will give you the keys of the kingdom of heaven; whatever you bind on earth will be bound in heaven, and whatever you loose on earth will be loosed in heaven" (Matthew 16:19).

15. exercising rulership

16. The King-Father has promised that once Lucifer and the kingdom of darkness are totally defeated by him, there will be a new heaven and earth ("Genesis II"), in which we will fully reflect the glory of the heavenly kingdom.

17. The fourth result of reconnection is a transformed outlook on life.

18. change

19. spirit; soul; body

20. Our outlook is to be transformed by a thorough understanding and reception of the mind and ways of the King, and through being receptive to the Governor's instructions and leading in our lives. The Governor changes our inner culture by teaching us a new way to live. He reveals to us the thoughts and ways of the King so that we may understand and follow them.

21. mind-set; lifestyle

22. The fifth result of reconnection is new courage and confidence.

23. The basis for our new courage and confidence is that there is nothing or no one in the world who has more power and resources than our King-Father. When the Spirit lives within us, heaven is our home country, and we have its authority and power. We do not need to be threatened by anyone on earth who tries to intimidate or harm us.

24. The fear of man is a snare to us as kingdom citizens because it will cause us to live by a mind-set and standards other than the kingdom's. We won't be acting in authority and power but in worry and timidity.

25. power; love; sound mind

26. The sixth result of a person being reconnected to the kingdom is a reconnection to his life purpose—to the assignment for which he was born.

27. A dream is something a person can see being accomplished in the future, even though he may not live to see it fully completed. A vision is something he can see to do, which he can complete in his lifetime.

28. The King planned for us to accomplish specific good works before we were born.

29. realms; giftings

30. True

31. The seventh result of reconnection is that the Governor gives us the ability to communicate with the heavenly government.

32. We can bring the kingdom of heaven to earth and have dominion only if we are receiving clear instructions from the King. A kingdom can function in delegated authority only if the purpose, will, and intent of the King are being transmitted to that delegated authority.

33. (1) Going to the King-Father through the King-Son, who opened the way for us by his substitutionary death; (2) going through the power of the Governor, who is our means of speaking with and hearing from the Father; relying on the Governor to communicate our requests and desires.

34. Worshipping the King is a form of communication with the heavenly government; it enables us to remain in right relationship with the King by keeping us in constant connection and communion with him and honoring his government; it protects us from establishing our own kingdoms on earth, rather than the heavenly government's, because we acknowledge and confirm to the King that his desires and will are paramount; through worship we affirm that the interests of the King's government are the ultimate reason for our existence.

Chapter Ten
THE NATURE OF THE GOVERNOR

1. Answers will vary.

2. misunderstood; ignored

3. (d) a distinct person with a personality

4. emotions

5. God; equal

6. By "God extended," Dr. Munroe means that the Holy Spirit is God extended to a person and/or situation to work the purpose and will of his kingdom in the person's life or in the circumstance.

7. personalities; dimensions

8. Dr. Munroe said it is the Holy Spirit who (1) convicts people of their need to be cleansed from sin by the work of Christ, and (2) enables us to be spiritually reborn and brings us into the heavenly kingdom. Therefore, if someone totally hardens himself to the Spirit and his work, he won't be drawn to forgiveness through Christ, and he won't be able to receive the regenerating work of the Spirit in his life.

9. A person has qualities and characteristics that distinguish him from others, so that he is a separate being. The Governor has a distinct personality, characteristics, and will. His main desire is for us to fulfill the King's purposes on earth.

10. The Holy Spirit has spiritual senses similar to the way human beings have physical senses. Spiritually speaking, the Holy Spirit sees, hears, feels, and smells or discerns in his dealings with the earth and its inhabitants.

11. Paul wrote, "Do not grieve the Holy Spirit of God, with whom you were sealed for the day of redemption" (Ephesians 4:30). We can grieve the Spirit when we actively resist him, behave in ways that are contrary to the kingdom of heaven, or neglect him.

12. When we neglect or ignore the Holy Spirit, he will sometimes withdraw our sense of his presence in order to get our attention.

13. We can learn to fellowship with and listen to the Holy Spirit by understanding that he speaks to us through the Scriptures, through our thoughts, and through promptings and impressions. We need to practice hearing his voice and not ignore him, but acknowledge him as a person who is intimately interested in who we are, what we do, and how we fulfill our role in the kingdom.

14. word; King

15. The first of the Holy Spirit's roles and responsibilities toward us is as our Counselor/Comforter.

16. The definition of the Greek word for Counselor, according to *Strong's* concordance, is "an intercessor, consoler," "advocate, comforter." Some Bible translations use the word "Helper." It refers to one who comes right alongside us to assist us.

17. Jesus used the analogy of a shepherd who leaves his ninety-nine sheep in the fold while he goes off to look for the one that is lost. See, for example, Luke 15:4–7.

18. The second of the Holy Spirit's roles and responsibilities toward us is as our Teacher/Guide.

19. The Governor is the only one who can enable us to understand the truth of the statements that Jesus made and the instructions he left for us. He is the only one who can reconnect us to original information about the King and his kingdom. He protects us from error and from others' opinions that are not according to the mind of the King. He reveals and explains the laws of the King to us, bringing those words to life.

20. The Governor makes us practical people in the world by showing us how to take our knowledge and apply it to life—by giving us wisdom. He shows us how to apply our knowledge to family, business, community, national, and worldwide issues.

21. The third of the Spirit's roles and responsibilities toward us is as our Helper/Enabler.

22. The first arena in which this help is given is in fulfilling the purposes of the kingdom on earth: telling the inhabitants about the promise of the Father, freeing them from the kingdom of darkness, and showing them the nature of the kingdom and how to enter in to it.

23. The second arena in which this help is given is in reconnecting us to our gifts. Every human being is born with gifts from God, but in order for these gifts to reach their maximum potential in service for the kingdom, they need to be reconnected to their original source. No one really knows the true essence of his gifts unless he reconnects with the Spirit of the Creator. Moreover, the Governor activates our gifts to a level that we wouldn't naturally bring them.

24. discern; understand; kingdom; created

25. purpose; potential

26. The two types of gifts are (1) the gifts we are born with; (2) additional gifts we are given when we receive the Spirit.

27. The gifts referred to in this chapter are the gifts we were born with to fulfill a specific purpose on earth for the kingdom.

28. The Holy Spirit does not necessarily give us the ability to *do* these gifts because that ability already exists within us. Rather, he empowers us by revealing them to us fully and introducing us to gifts we didn't even know we had. Moreover, he shows us how to use them for the kingdom rather than for selfish purposes.

29. The fourth of the Holy Spirit's roles and responsibilities toward us is as our Convicter.

30. The Governor convicts those outside the kingdom that they need to be forgiven and connected to their Father in the heavenly government.

31. The Governor convicts the citizens of the kingdom of attitudes and actions that are contrary to the nature of the kingdom. He makes all the citizens conscious of the expectations, the standards, the laws, the regulations, and the customs of the kingdom, and he convinces them of the benefits of these things. He works through their consciences so they will choose to live according to kingdom standards.

32. prompts; desire; desires

33. The fifth of the Holy Spirit's roles and responsibilities toward us is as Drawer to God.

34. The Governor draws people to God in a gentle way. Hosea 11:4 says, "I led them with cords of human kindness, with ties of love."

35. The sixth of the Holy Spirit's roles and responsibilities toward us is as Communicator.

36. The Governor's words will never disagree with the King's words or bring a message that is contrary to them. He will remind us of what the King has already said and what he desires, and he will also speak prophetically of the future of the kingdom.

37. The seventh of the Holy Spirit's roles and responsibilities toward us is as our Sanctifier.

38. As Sanctifier, the Governor helps free us from things in our lives that are contrary to the nature of the King and that diminish our capacity to maximize our gifts for the kingdom. He eliminates hindrances to our development and progress. The separation involves some painful "winnowing," but it is for our benefit. The King doesn't want anything to stop us from fulfilling our potential and accomplishing our purpose.

39. The Governor also sanctifies us in the sense of setting us apart for the service of the heavenly kingdom, and for the day when the King will once more return to the earth to live forever with his people with the creation of a new heaven and earth. It is the Holy Spirit's job to prepare every aspect of our lives for the King's coming.

Chapter Eleven
THE GOVERNOR'S CULTURE

1. Answers will vary.

2. National character is defined as the combination of a country's beliefs, attitudes, values, conventions, practices, and characteristics.

3. In a kingdom, the monarch's character and characteristics were vastly important because they influenced and often determined the state of the environment over which he ruled. They created what life was like in the kingdom.

4. The key to a successful kingdom is the good character of its king.

5. character; environment; king

6. The King wants us to understand the nature of his kingdom, so that we can trust it and what it means to live in it.

7. Jesus said, "You know that the rulers of the Gentiles lord it over them, and their high officials exercise authority over them. Not so with you. Instead, whoever wants to become great among you must be your servant, and whoever wants to be first must be your slave—just as the Son of Man did not come to be served, but to serve, and to give his life as a ransom for many" (Matthew 20:25–28). Answers regarding this statement's central theme may vary, but it may be summed up as "servant leadership."

8. Paul listed the qualities of love, joy, peace, patience, kindness, goodness, faithfulness, gentleness, and self-control.

9. evident; present

10. Paul used this particular analogy of fruit because fruit doesn't appear overnight; it develops over time, and he wanted them to know that they would have to *cultivate* the culture of the King in their lives, under the example and leading of the Governor.

11. You develop this seed by putting into your life the kingdom elements that allow it to grow. The spiritual nutrients that enable the fruit to grow in our lives are maintaining a continual connection with the King, learning the Constitution of the kingdom (the Scripture) and yielding to the direction of the Governor in our lives.

12. natural; nature

13. The way you behave, the way you respond to others, the way you react to problems, and the way you deal with disappointments should all reveal the culture of heaven. The qualities of the Spirit within you define the uniqueness of your nature. Your unique nature then links you to your heavenly heritage.

14. (a) uncomfortable and unnatural

15. The invisible kingdom of God lives within you through the presence of the Governor. The human kingdom, the kingdom of darkness fueled by Lucifer, is all around you. In addition, remnants of the rebellious nature are still present in your life and need to be rooted out.

16. Paul wrote to the Philippians that we are to keep our focus on the heavenly kingdom because "our citizenship is in heaven." (See Philippians 3:7–15, 20.) He told the Galatians, "Those who belong to Christ Jesus have crucified the sinful nature with its passions and desires. Since we live by the Spirit, let us keep in step with the Spirit" (Galatians 5:24–25). The disciple John encouraged kingdom citizens, "The one who is in you is greater than the one who is in the world" (1 John 4:4). In other words, the power of the Governor within you exponentially exceeds the power of the kingdom of the world around you.

17. False. (The true statement is, The culture of heaven and the culture of the world are opposites; you cannot experience the kingdom of heaven if you are living according to a foreign culture.)

18. The Governor rebukes and corrects us in two ways: (1) he uses the internal warning system of our consciences; (2) he reminds us of the teachings of the King. He brings to our minds what is recorded in the Constitution of the kingdom, or the written record of the King's words and ways, the Scriptures.

19. changed; follow

20. The Governor has the challenging job of teaching us to be what we were originally created to be.

21. Because of humanity's rebellion, we lost our capacity to manifest the King's nature. That nature has been distorted in us because of our former association with the kingdom of darkness. The Governor therefore begins by teaching us to relate to the Creator as our Father again, so that we can call him, "Abba, Father," just as the King-Son did. This relationship enables us to be remade in the image of our Creator.

22. does; is; essence

23. We are to carefully watch what we allow to enter the personal culture of our spirits, souls, and bodies.

24. mansion; clean

25. Being a kingdom citizen requires that we exist in some degree of tension because we live in the midst of a culture of rebellion and death. This is especially so because our old culture is fighting with the demands of the new culture.

26. We remain on earth and in this tension for the purpose of spreading the kingdom of light and pushing back the kingdom of darkness.

27. Even as we live in this tension, therefore, we live in the reality of the love, joy, peace, patience, kindness, goodness, faithfulness, gentleness, and self-control of the heavenly kingdom.

28. character; power

29. Character develops over time, but ability-power from the Governor can be received immediately after a person realigns with the King and receives the outpouring of the Spirit in his life.

30. Character is more important than power because it protects our use of that power. It keeps us from using it for the wrong motivations and purposes. It prevents us from using our power to hurt others rather than to help them. We must develop the fruit—such as love, kindness, and self-control—because they will moderate our use of the gifts. Power without character is dangerous.

31. ongoing; lifelong

32. influence; influence; kingdom

Chapter Twelve
MANIFESTING KINGDOM CULTURE

1. Answers will vary.

2. (1) Land (territory); (2) Culture (what the nation stands for; its ideals); (3) Values (the standards the people of the nation live by); (4) Language (a common form of communication)

3. language

4. Language is the key to national identity.

5. contained

6. Language creates national unity.

7. unity; break down

8. Language is the key to effective communication.

9. A common language transmits essential national culture, values, history, goals, needs, and desires to current and subsequent generations.

10. Language is the key to effective expression.

11. Lacking the ability to articulate what you desire to say makes it difficult for people to participate in a nation as full-fledged citizens.

12. Language signifies a common heritage.

13. generational transfer; family heritage

14. When human beings rebelled against their King and lost the Governor, the clear lines of communication between the heavenly kingdom and the inhabitants on earth were disrupted. In this sense, we could say that heaven and earth no longer had a "common language."

15. Answers may vary somewhat, but essentially human beings were using their common language to continue to disassociate themselves from the King. Out of pride, they wanted to build a tower to make a name for themselves—for their own honor and glory—without acknowledging and giving due honor to the King. The tower became like an idol to them. Whatever is not for God's glory will eventually be to our detriment. Having a common language was a powerful tool that, if left unchecked, would lead humanity even further down the road in their rebellion and separation from the King. Therefore, the King caused the people to speak different languages to confuse them. The building of the tower was halted, and the people were divided according to language.

16. protecting; restore; return

17. One of the first things the Governor gives us after we receive his infilling is the ability to speak in heaven-given languages.

18. (1) an earthly language, but one the speaker does not understand; (2) a heavenly language that is unknown on earth

19. Through heaven-given languages, the Governor enables human beings to once more share a "common tongue" with the heavenly King.

20. Jesus said, "These signs will accompany those who believe: In my name they will drive out demons; *they will speak in new tongues*;…they will place their hands on sick people, and they will get well" (Mark 16:17–18, emphasis added).

21. language; power

22. This event was a sign of the fulfillment of the King's promise. It showed that the communication lines between heaven and earth were open once more through the return of the Governor. It was also an indication that God desired to restore unity among the people of the world.

23. At the incident of the Tower of Babel, God confused the people with multiple languages so he could weaken them. At Pentecost, he gave his people the gift of languages in order

to strengthen them in their new kingdom life, as well as enable them to communicate the promise of the Spirit to other inhabitants on earth who needed to hear this message.

24. identity

25. Speaking in tongues gives direct communication with the King.

26. When we find it difficult to pray in our earthly language, the Governor speaks for us and through us to the Father, through spiritual communication. Paul wrote, "The Spirit helps us in our weakness. We do not know what we ought to pray for, but the Spirit himself intercedes for us with groans that words cannot express. And he who searches our hearts knows the mind of the Spirit, because the Spirit intercedes for the saints in accordance with God's will" (Romans 8:26–27).

27. Speaking in tongues is a sign we are connected with the King.

28. evidence; citizenship

29. If we realize that tongues are what comes natural to citizens of the kingdom, their strangeness disappears and their true purpose becomes clear.

30. Tongues were given to kingdom citizens to assist them in kingdom purposes, and we are still living in a time when we need this assistance on earth. Their value to the first-century kingdom citizens is their value to us today—communication with the King-Father as we carry out his will in the world.

31. Dr. Munroe said heaven-given languages are a powerful unifier among those who have received them, and this is why Lucifer fights against the baptism in the Holy Spirit and the outpouring of heavenly gifts to the children of the King. Lucifer encourages some kingdom citizens to create doctrines against the gift of tongues; in this way he tries to make sure that not all kingdom citizens will speak a common, unifying "language."

32. If you do not speak in tongues, you will have problems communicating with the kingdom, and you will lack the power you could have in living the kingdom life.

33. direct

34. (1) tongues for direct, personal communication with the King; (2) tongues for corporate communication

35. The first type of tongues is for individual edification. The second type of tongues is not for individuals but for the building up of all those gathered in an assembly of kingdom citizens. It involves the public declaration of the King's will and words of encouragement, given in a heaven-given language or languages, through someone whom the Governor helps to speak the mind of the King. This is accompanied by an interpretation of the King's message in the language of the people who are gathered, to assure that everyone understands it.

36. releasing; using

37. The first reason for speaking in tongues is that they are a sign of connection to the kingdom; they are often the initial supernatural evidence of the indwelling and filling of the Spirit.

38. builds up; recharges

39. The third reason for speaking in tongues is that it reminds us of the Governor's indwelling presence; when we are conscious of his presence, we are encouraged and comforted.

40. (c) keep our prayers in line with God's will

41. stimulate faith

42. The sixth reason for speaking in tongues is to keep us free from worldly contamination. Tongues keep us in constant connection with the culture of the kingdom, even as we live in the midst of the culture of the world.

43. unknown

44. spiritual refreshing

45. The ninth reason for speaking in tongues is to help us in giving thanks.

46. The tenth reason for speaking in tongues is to bring the tongue under subjection.

47. tongues; control; Spirit

48. Through tongues, the Governor communicates our requests to the King, and the King's will to us. We can't pray effectively without the Governor, because he knows the mind of the King and how our requests fit with the purposes of the kingdom.

Chapter Thirteen
THE GOVERNOR'S ADMINISTRATION

1. Answers will vary.

2. The Governor is responsible for training kingdom citizens on earth in how to have dominion in the territory.

3. The gifts of the Spirit are the delegation and distribution of powers by the Governor to kingdom citizens, in order to execute government business in the colony. They are for the purpose of *impacting* the earthly environment.

4. When the King-Son was on earth, he healed people, cast out demons, and did miracles. He did *practical* works on earth; he went about solving people's problems through the power of the Governor.

5. wills. Paul wrote in the Constitution of the kingdom, "All these [gifts of the Spirit] are the work of one and the same Spirit, and he gives them to each one, *just as he determines*" (1 Corinthians 12:11, emphasis added).

6. False. (The real answer is that authorized power is given for the service of the heavenly kingdom.)

7. As the Governor delegates kingdom authority to us, he teaches us how to administer his gifts correctly and effectively. He teaches us directly and through the Constitution of the kingdom (the Scriptures).

8. Administration of the gifts has to do with serving others, not lording it over them. The Constitution of the kingdom says, "Each one should use whatever gift he has received *to serve others*, faithfully *administering* God's grace in its various forms" (1 Peter 4:10, emphasis added), and "Now to each one *the manifestation of the Spirit is given for the common good*" (1 Corinthians 12:7, emphasis added).

9. property

10. When people believe that the power they have been authorized to use comes from their own abilities, rather than directly from the Governor, this leads to their using the power for their own purposes, such as boosting their egos, making money, or exercising control over others. This is dangerous for both the people abusing the power and the ones they are supposed to be serving. They fail to fulfill their call, and the people who are meant to benefit from their service go without the help they could have received.

11. needs; greatest impact

12. people; environment

13. Spiritual gifts that are in the form of specific roles are for building up all citizens in the kingdom.

14. The authorized power given by the Governor to kingdom citizens equips them to deal with conflict and opposition from the kingdom of darkness, which exists not to benefit, but to destroy, the inhabitants of earth.

15. (1) Gifts that say something, or gifts of utterance: prophecy, different kinds of tongues, and the interpretation of tongues; (2) gifts that do something, or gifts of power: faith, miraculous powers or the working of miracles, and gifts of healing; (3) gifts that reveal something, or gifts of revelation: the message or word of wisdom, the message or word of knowledge, and distinguishing or discerning between spirits

16. variety; unity

17. The revelation gifts address such things as facts, events, purpose, motivation, destiny,

and whether something is human, whether it is of the kingdom of heaven, or whether it is of the kingdom of darkness.

18. The message or word of wisdom is a supernatural revelation by the Holy Spirit concerning the mind and will of God and his divine purposes. It is authorized power from the Governor that gives kingdom citizens the ability to know the best thing to do in difficult or perplexing situations.

19. A word of supernatural wisdom is different from wisdom obtained through a knowledge of the Scriptures in that it comes directly from the King to a citizen (or citizens) through the Governor, enabling him to deal judiciously in the affairs of life.

20. Scriptural accounts reveal this wisdom may come in the form of a vision, a dream, an angel (messenger) from the King, or a word or impression given to a kingdom citizen by the Governor.

21. A word of wisdom may apply to the person who receives it or to someone else.

22. apply; policy; purposes

23. While wisdom is about application, knowledge is about having the *information* you need to make the best decisions in executing delegated authority in the colony. It refers to the government providing you with the ability to understand its policies; but especially, it gives you the ability to understand what the King is thinking—it is supernatural revelation by the Governor of certain facts in the mind of the King.

24. The word of knowledge may be manifested through an inward revelation, the interpretation of tongues, a word of prophecy, a vision, or an angel.

25. True

26. Acts 11:27–30 tells about a prophet named Agabus who was given a word of knowledge that a severe famine would afflict the entire Roman world. The kingdom citizens took this knowledge and applied it [wisdom], deciding to send relief to kingdom citizens living in Judea.

27. The authorized power of faith is a supernatural belief or confidence. It is the government providing its citizens with special ability to believe in its policies—to know without a doubt that a particular outcome will ultimately be manifested for the purposes of the kingdom—so they will take action to carry them out.

28. Faith that comes through exposure to and application of the Scriptures is (1) faith with which we enter the kingdom through belief in the sacrifice of the King-Son on our behalf, and the forgiveness we receive as a result; (2) the fruit of the Spirit known as "faithfulness"; (3) the faith by which kingdom believers daily live as they trust the King to carry out his purposes through their lives and to bring them encouragement and peace.

29. The working of miracles.

30. Gifts of healing are supernatural cures for disease and disability. No natural means are involved, whether medical science or other forms of the application of human knowledge.

31. welfare; securing; welfare

32. The plural usage refers to the ability to heal different kinds of diseases. The book of Matthew records, "Jesus was going about in all Galilee, teaching in their synagogues, and proclaiming the gospel of the kingdom, and healing *every kind of disease* and *every kind of sickness* among the people" (Matthew 4:23 NASB, emphasis added).

33. The gifts of healing address a variety of sickness, both mental and physical, that bring us into disharmony with ourselves, other people, or the King-Father. This would include things such as fear, loneliness, and depression.

34. Supernatural healing comes from another world—the heavenly kingdom; the care of a physician only *assists* the healing ability that our Creator has placed within our own bodies; and the body's natural ability to heal is an inbuilt capacity.

35. Gifts of healing are manifested through a kingdom citizen to whom the Governor gives a special administration of healing; they occur through the activity of a kingdom citizen as empowered by the Governor. A healing that occurs through a person's faith in God's promises comes about when the person applies to himself statements about the King's desire to heal us, such as this one: "He himself bore our sins in his body on the tree, so that we might die to sins and live for righteousness; by his wounds you have been healed" (1 Peter 2:24).

36. Sympathy means that you feel sorry for the person, empathize with his illness, and want to help him. Compassion, however, is an almost irresistible urge to free a person from the sickness or problem afflicting him. There is true passion in com*passion* that alleviates suffering.

37. In the administration of the kingdom of heaven on earth, the gifts of healing are the Governor's authorization of kingdom citizens to free others from being invaded by anything that is abnormal to the kingdom. In this way, the government shows evidence that it is present and can address negative conditions in the colony. In the kingdom of God, healing is executing justice. The Governor confirms the rights of the citizens to live in wholeness.

38. In one sense, all gifts of the Spirit are miracles because they are beyond our natural experience. But miraculous powers or the working of miracles are specific acts that defy human understanding. A miracle is a supernatural intervention in the ordinary course of nature, a temporary suspension in the accustomed order of things by an act of the Spirit of God.

39. In the administration of the kingdom of heaven on earth, miracles are the government providing for the special needs of people. Whatever the miracle is, whether it is supplying food, raising the dead, or something else, it is provision. Miracles are not entertainment; they are the result of the Governor, through citizens under his authority, performing actions that confirm the presence of the kingdom and its ability to transform the environment of the colony.

40. Prophecy is a message from the King, supernaturally given, in an earthly language known to the hearer or hearers. It is the heavenly government giving its citizens confirmation about information the government has previously told them.

41. edification; exhortation; consolation; comfort

42. strengthening; building; ways

43. (b) earnestly sought

44. misused

45. The gift of prophecy is about *forth*telling, or declaring the will of the King, while the office of prophet also includes *fore*telling, or the government giving a citizen the ability to receive news before it happens. This may be an announcement of what the King plans to do in the future. A prophet usually has other revelation gifts operating in his life, as well, such as the word of knowledge or wisdom, or the discerning of spirits. Just because someone exercises the gift of prophecy, this doesn't necessarily mean this is his regular position or responsibility on behalf of the heavenly government. It just means he has been given special information from the King at that particular time. When people try to prophesy in an unauthorized way, this leads to confusion and an abuse of the gift.

46. The authorized power of prophecy is the Governor providing a kingdom citizen with information that supports and encourages his fellow citizens in the life of the kingdom. It is a reminder to kingdom citizens that the heavenly government is still at work on their behalf, no matter what they might be going through. Everything they need is on the way—whether it's deliverance, freedom, peace, or healing.

47. Distinguishing between spirits or the discerning of spirits gives a kingdom citizen insight into the supernatural world and its workings. Its revelation is focused on a single class of beings, spirits, and should not be confused with discernment that comes as a result of a word of wisdom.

48. (d) discerning both good and evil nonhuman spiritual beings

49. messages; impressions

50. visible likeness

51. source

52. The authorized power of discernment often works in conjunction with the word of wisdom or the word of knowledge.

53. In terms of kingdom administration, the gift of discernment is the government giving a kingdom citizen sensitivity to the supernatural environment around him.

54. Different kinds of tongues are supernatural utterances given by the Holy Spirit in languages not necessarily understood by the speaker or hearer. They are either expressions from the Governor to the King on behalf of the citizens, or expressions from the King through the Governor in response to the citizens.

55. private; oneself; public; others

56. The gift of different kinds of tongues is manifested within a gathering of kingdom citizens. It is given by the Governor to whom he wills, for the benefit of all citizens.

57. The authorized power of special tongues should be exercised according to the following guidelines: (1) tongues are not to be expressed continuously or at exactly the same time as others but in sequence; (2) tongues should be spoken in a given meeting by only two or three people; (3) tongues should not be spoken out loud if there is no one to interpret; (4) the person giving the tongue can pray to receive an interpretation of it; (5) a person who receives an interpretation shouldn't wait for another to speak it (unless someone else is already speaking), but should faithfully deliver the interpretation so as not to cause others to miss a word from the King; (6) a prophecy may sometimes follow tongues.

58. Tongues are not to be spoken out loud in a meeting of kingdom citizens unless there is interpretation because no one will understand the message or be edified by it (say "Amen" to it).

59. If the gift of tongues is working in you, you may feel an intense interest in and compassion for the people around you. Some of the words may start forming in your mind. You might even almost be able to "see" the words in your mind's eye, or "feel" the words coming. You then speak them on the basis of your faith in the government's communication and your yieldedness to the Governor's prompting.

60. (c) build people up

61. True

62. The gift of special tongues sometimes takes the form of earthly language(s) that those outside the kingdom can understand in order to draw them to the King for reconciliation.

63. Tongues are the heavenly government giving a kingdom citizen the ability to communicate its policies, wishes, and intents to both citizens of the kingdom and other inhabitants of the earth.

64. The power of interpretation of tongues is manifested when the Governor reveals to a kingdom citizen the meaning of an utterance spoken in special tongues, and the person speaks that interpretation to the assembly.

65. False. (This is not a word-for-word translation but an interpretation that makes the communication comprehensible in the human language of the citizens. An utterance in a heaven-given language may lead to an interpretation of longer or shorter length than the original utterance.)

66. The purpose of interpretation of tongues is to render the meaning of tongues intelligible to the hearers so that the whole assembly of kingdom citizens can be instructed, warned, strengthened, or encouraged by it.

67. baptism

Chapter Fourteen
WHY THE WHOLE WORLD NEEDS THE GOVERNOR

1. Answers will vary.

2. Answers will vary.

3. self-generated

4. Our world needs relevant, practical, and effective help from another world.

5. immediately relevant to the world we live in

6. We will continue to be victims of our own corrupt nature if the people of our nations, the individuals we appoint as leaders over us, and the institutions of our societies do not have a higher source of reference for their convictions, beliefs, morals, values, and standards.

7. The Creator-King's design for humankind's life on earth requires that human beings be filled with the very Spirit of the Creator himself—the Holy Spirit—the Governor of heaven.

8. False. The person and role of the Holy Spirit is not a religious issue, but a social, economic, cultural, and political concern. The Holy Spirit is therefore a national and international issue.

9. life, purpose, and effectiveness

10. The King's plan is for a *community* of kings and priests who will reign on earth.

11. Governor

12. Corporately, the world has rejected the presence and influence of the Governor. Consequently, we experience wars, natural disasters, and social crises on earth.

13. When a community of kings and priests works together for the right reasons—honoring and expressing the nature of our King—and acts in genuine unity, we will have powerful potential to influence the earth with the nature of the kingdom.

14. The heavenly government provides for, encourages, and enables the fulfillment of the greatest individual and corporate potential in life.

15. The King's attitude toward his citizens is one of great love and a desire for their highest good in life.

16. Lucifer would like to perpetuate the sorrow and darkness of the world so that he can continue to control it. He desires to consolidate the people of the world under his harsh rule so they can never become free.

17. The King-Son destroyed Satan's power over the world, transferring us from being under the darkness of a corrupt world into the light of the heavenly kingdom.

18. The message of Jesus and the Scriptures is the presence of the kingdom of heaven on earth, through the Holy Spirit's return.

19. Humanity's collective purpose and calling is exercising kingdom dominion on earth, under the guidance of the Governor.

20. As we yield to the Governor's presence and work in our lives, we will spread the kingdom of God on earth. Change will take place in all areas of life and in people of all national and ethnic backgrounds, East and West; and from all social and economic circumstances. People will be transformed according to the heavenly kingdom, so that life, and not confusion, stress, and death, will be the result.

21. life; fullest

22. The King's plan for the complete transformation of the world into his image and nature will climax in the creation of a new heaven and earth. In effect, heaven and earth will become one, so that there will be no essential distinction between the two, and God himself will live among his people. The creation of a new heaven and earth will be the apex of the plan of the King for the coming of the Governor, which he had in mind from the beginning. The kingdom of darkness will be completely destroyed. The people of earth will be a true world community of kings and priests living out the kingdom life in its fullness.

23. key

24. The Holy Spirit is the most important person on earth because he brings us the presence and power of the kingdom of heaven.

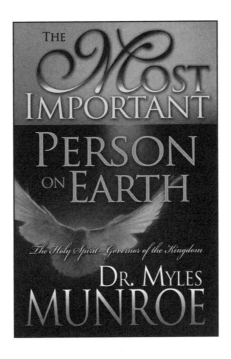

The Most Important Person on Earth:
The Holy Spirit, Governor of the Kingdom
Dr. Myles Munroe

The Holy Spirit is not only the most important Person on earth—he's also the most important Person you'll ever know. Meet him in the pages of this book, and discover why he is the key to your purpose and fulfillment in life.

In *The Most Important Person on Earth*, Dr. Myles Munroe explains how the Holy Spirit is the Governor of God's kingdom on earth, much as royal governors administered the will of earthly kings in their territories. Under the guidance and enabling of the Holy Spirit, you will discover how to bring order to the chaos in your life, receive God's power to heal and deliver, fulfill your true purpose with joy, become a leader in your sphere of influence, and be part of God's government on earth. Enter into the fullness of God's Spirit as you embrace God's design for your life today.

ISBN: 978-0-88368-986-8 • Hardcover • 320 pages

www.whitakerhouse.com

Whether you are a businessperson, a student, a homemaker, or a head of state, Dr. Myles Munroe explains how you can make your dreams and hopes a living reality. Your success is not dependent on the state of the economy or what the job market is like. You do not need to be hindered by the limited perceptions of others or by a lack of resources. Revive your passion for living, pursue your dream, discover your vision—and find your true life.

The Principles and Power of Vision
Dr. Myles Munroe
ISBN: 978-0-88368-951-6 • Hardcover • 240 pages

While all people possess leadership potential, many do not understand how to cultivate the leadership nature and how to apply it to their lives. Discover the unique attitudes that all effective leaders exhibit, how to eliminate hindrances to your leadership abilities, and how to fulfill your particular calling in life. With wisdom and power, Dr. Munroe reveals a wealth of practical insights that will move you from being a follower to becoming the leader you were meant to be!

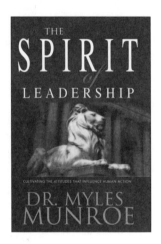

The Spirit of Leadership
Dr. Myles Munroe
ISBN: 978-0-88368-983-7 • Hardcover • 304 pages

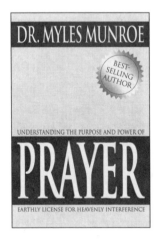

God, God Almighty, God the Creator of man—this same God, in all His power and all His majesty, stops and listens when you pray. All that God is—and all that God has—may be received through prayer. Everything you need to fulfill your purpose on earth is available to you through prayer. Dr. Myles Munroe takes the mystery out of prayer, providing practical answers for difficult questions about communicating with God. Be prepared to enter into a new dimension of faith and a deeper revelation of God's love for you.

Understanding the Purpose and Power of Prayer
Dr. Myles Munroe
ISBN: 978-0-88368-442-9 • Trade • 240 pages

www.whitakerhouse.com